HOLY WIND

in NAVAJO PHILOSOPHY

There was a time when every gazing hill
Was holy with the wonder that it saw,
And every valley was a place of awe,
And what the grass knew never could be told.

John G. Neihardt
A Cycle of the West

Holy Wind in NAVAJO PHILOSOPHY

James Kale McNeley

THE UNIVERSITY OF ARIZONA PRESS
Tucson

About the author . . .

JAMES KALE MCNELEY began his association with the Navajo at mid-century when he came to New Mexico to work as a social caseworker on the Navajo reservation. Before coming to the Southwest he studied psychology and social sciences at Drake University, Columbia University, and the New School for Social Research and worked as a social worker in New York City. After receiving his Ph.D. in Psychological Anthropology from the University of Hawaii he became a teacher, alongside his wife, a Navajo, at the Shiprock campus of Navajo Community College.

Seventh printing 2009

THE UNIVERSITY OF ARIZONA PRESS
© 1981 The Arizona Board of Regents
All rights reserved

www.uapress.arizona.edu

Library of Congress Cataloging-in-Publication Data
McNeley, James Kale.
  Holy wind in Navajo philosophy.

  Bibliography: p.
  Includes index.
  1. Navaho Indians—Religion and Mythology.
2. Navaho Indians—Philosophy. 3. Indians of
North America—Southwest, New—Religion and
mythology. 4. Indians of North America—Southwest,
New—Philosophy. I. Title.
E99.N3M317   299′.78   80-27435
ISBN 0-8165-0710-4
ISBN 0-8165-0724-4 (pbk.)

Manufactured in the United States of America on acid-free, archival-quality paper and processed chlorine free.

This book was set in 10/12 V-I-P Palatino.

*To my parents and teachers and
to the singers who informed this
book with their knowledge*

CONTENTS

PREFACE

The study of *Holy Wind in Navajo Philosophy* is based on a combination of field interviews with Navajo informants and library research, both conducted during 1970–1972 from a base at Many Farms, Arizona, in the central part of the Navajo Nation. Data analysis involving Navajo research assistants was conducted at the same site.

Informants were sought who were believed to be especially knowledgeable about traditional Navajo culture. Among the Navajo, singers who are practitioners of the various ceremonials and healing chants, are known to be primary bearers of traditional lore, being well-versed in the general origin myth as well as in specialty myths which branch off at various points. Of the ten informants used in this study, eight were, or had been, practicing singers (all but CL and JD). No effort was made to control for these singers' specialties; however, when the importance of the Wind concept in Navajo psychology became apparent, informants who were practitioners of the Navajo Windway ceremonial were chosen (these being informants FDT and BY). Of the two informants who were not practicing singers, CL claimed a knowledge and practice of divination procedures and JD asserted knowledge of the Chiricahua Windway ceremonial.

In selecting informants care was also given to choose those who would be expected to be least influenced in their views by acculturation processes. Eight of the ten informants were over 60 years of age at the time of the study and six of these fell between the ages of 75 and 94 years (informants CM, CAB, GES, FDT, HB, and HK). All but one (JD) were monolingual Navajo speakers and lacking in significant formal education in Anglo schools. JD had a limited knowledge of conversational English. All informants, excepting JD who was visiting from Shiprock, New Mexico, resided in the general area of the Chinle Valley of the Navajo Nation within an area accessible from Many Farms, Arizona.

Interviews, which were conducted with the aid of an interpreter, usually began with very general, open-ended questions such as, "What makes people behave the way they do?" Informants were given the opportunity to respond freely and expansively. They would not uncommonly refer to the oral traditions and recite long passages of mythology appropriate to the particular question. Following the narration of such texts, informants were asked more specific questions to clarify their responses or to elicit interpretive statements, "folk definitions" of terms, and other data that are not generally embedded within the oral literature itself.

Informants interviewed by the author are referred to throughout this book by initials. By way of contrast, statements that are attributed to the informants of other writers are generally indicated by giving the name rather than the initials of the informant followed by the usual citations made to published works.

In selecting published versions of Navajo myths for review, priority was given to those versions judged by earlier investigators to be the most complete and of highest quality, those transcribed in Navajo with interlinear translations into English, and versions expected to help explicate the role of Winds in Navajo ideology. It should be noted that it is not within the limits of this study to make a comprehensive presentation, review, or analysis of the entire origin myth or of other Navajo myths. Myth segments were selected to the degree that they were anticipated to contribute towards an understanding of the Navajo Wind concept and related concepts of the determinants of thought and behavior. In accordance with the above criteria, the versions of Navajo origin myths by Matthews (1897), Curtis (1907), Franciscan Fathers (1910), Stephen (1930), Goddard (1933), Klah (1942), Fishler (1953), O'Bryan (1956), and Haile (n.d. *b*) were reviewed. On the subject of the Blessingway myth, three sources by Haile (1932*a*, 1930, n.d. *a*) and one by Wyman (1970) were selected. For the chantway myths, the sources were Haile (1932*b*, 1932*c*, 1933*a*, 1933*b*), Wheelwright (1949), and Wyman (1962).

Precautions were taken to best assure that the Navajo point of view would be discerned and faithfully presented, particularly in a study such as this of a non-Western conception of personality. Evans-Pritchard, in his foreword to the 1971 edition of Lévy-Bruhl's *The "Soul" of the Primitive,* accurately characterized the difficulty of arriving at an understanding of such conceptions:

> We are dealing with conceptions such as those which we translate as "soul" and "spirit." That is as near as we can get to their meaning in our own language, but what the words in their own languages mean to those who speak them may not correspond exactly, or even at all, with what the words by which we translate them mean to us. In the process of translation, or mistranslation, we may easily put into the thought of primitive people ideas quite foreign to them. . . . (LévyBruhl 1971 [1927]:6)

Lévy-Bruhl's recommendations for coping with such difficulties appear in the same volume:

> It is essential to address one's questions only to the informed natives who are thoroughly conversant with the traditions and ceremonies of their group, to secure their whole-hearted sincerity by winning their confidence and liking, and lastly, to take down their testimony in their own language, before risking a translation which may not be exact, since the native words and phrases very often have no satisfactory equivalents in our European language. (Levy-Bruhl 1971 [1927]:201)

The importance of recording native views in their own languages when investigating philosophical formulations in traditional societies was also emphasized by Radin (1957 [1927]:xxx). The use of the native text for the analysis of meaning of elements in that text is recognized, as well, in theories of semantics that conceive of a term's meaning as existing in its system of relationships with other terms in the language; therefore, only by examining the use made of the terms in utterances is it possible to gain knowledge of a concept held by others (Lyons 1968:411). For Werner and others, the meaning of a term is to be found in its sense relationships with other terms with which it may combine in culturally true sentences (Werner et al. 1969:13, 95–96).

Consistent with the above precepts, the recording and analysis of Navajo texts became an essential part of the methodology of this study. In attempting to grasp traditional Navajo conceptions of human life and behavior, the direct objects of study are Navajo terms and utterances employed by native speakers in talking about such life and behavior. Inclusion of Navajo texts in the appendix reflects its methodological importance and documents translations and interpretations. Numbered citations to the Navajo texts are made throughout this work at the end of English translations of informants' statements. Hopefully these data will prove to be useful to other students of the Navajo and, as well, will be of interest and use to that growing body of Navajo students who have a reading command of their language and an interest in their traditional culture.

Variations between the statements of informants and between one myth version and another, as well as variations in interpretation and translation by Navajo research assistants, posed various methodological problems in defining Navajo beliefs. Some of these variations can be attributed to the ways in which the aspect of cultural knowledge dealt with in this study is learned and transmitted to others. Navajo sacred lore and associated beliefs are customarily learned from an older relative or, particularly when it is learned in conjunction with the learning of a ritual, from a singer to whom one may be apprenticed. Such knowledge is considered to be valuable property that is not freely shared with others in ordinary discourse. Each informant, then, was the recipient of a particular oral tradition. For this reason variations between informants in the statement and interpretation of beliefs are to be expected as among any other people whose histories and belief systems rest upon privately relayed oral traditions.

There are also sociolinguistic factors that are important in influencing the Navajo retelling of myths. Among these conditions are the suitability of the audience as recipients of sacred knowledge (Navajo narrators of myths will frequently acknowledge that they are omitting portions because of this consideration); the lack of time or inclination to tell the histories in their complete complexity and detail; the purpose of the narration and the expressed interests of the listener; the quality of the relationship between the historian and his listener; and, the amount and kind of remuneration offered. Such problems are augmented by disparities in knowledge of traditional culture on the part of the Navajo research assistants who assisted in the interviews and in transcribing and translating the tapes. Most of these younger, bilingual Navajos indicated that significant parts of what was told by informants had not previously been known to them. Certain words and phrases used by informants were unfamiliar to them so that recourse was sometimes made to Navajo-English dictionaries as a means of establishing the sense of such items. These factors contributed to variations in the translation of Navajo terms and in the interpretation of informants' beliefs while at the same time indicating that the beliefs described in this study are, in part, restricted to the more knowledgeable of the bearers of traditional lore. In dealing with such problems, the search for areas of consensus or agreement between informants was enhanced by the use of term concordances. In bringing together the utterances of different informants in relationship to key terms, their statements could be compared in such a way as to facilitate the discovery of regularities in the meanings of Navajo terms and in beliefs.

The interviewing and literature review procedures outlined above, and the recording of Navajo texts, provided large amounts of linguistic data pertaining to Navajo concepts and beliefs. A method was required for collating related statements from diverse sources, eliminating redundant statements, and discovering relationships between different parts of the whole regardless of original source or context; that is, a method for reducing the corpus of sentences ". . . to a smaller body of propositions that the sentences can be said to represent or embody" (Kay 1966:108–109).

The term concordance method was used for these purposes. With the assistance of Navajo helpers relevant statements were extracted from taped recordings of interviews with informants and were recorded in quadruple in written Navajo together with interlinear as well as free translations into English. In a similar manner, relevant sections of previously recorded mythological texts were extracted and recorded in quadruple. These multiple transcriptions provided the means by which diverse usages of commonly appearing terms could be brought together or concorded, providing naturally occurring linguistic contexts for the semantic analysis and interpretation of lexical items (the theoretical and methodological bases for the use of concordances in semantic studies are found in Werner 1967 and Werner et al. 1969). Thus, for example, the category of *nìłch'i hwii'siziinii* (initially translated as "the in-standing Wind Soul") in the concordance files contains sentences from diverse sources embedding this term in different contexts each of which, through predicating relationships to other Navajo terms, helps to establish the term's meaning. A sentence from one source clarifies one aspect of the term's meaning while that from some other source clarifies another. The following are free translations of a few of the many sentences under the concordance entry for "the in-standing Wind":

> There is just one standing within us by means of which we talk. It derives from them (the four Winds of the cardinal directions). (CAB)
> The one that stands within us sticks out of our earfolds. (BY)
> This one who is reckless and who talks just any way has faults. The one that stands within him leads him to think in that way, it seems. (FDT)

In instances in which a sentence from a given source seemingly contradicts that from another source or is contrary to the prevailing interpretation of the term, a clue is thereby provided that additional exploration is needed or that the prevailing interpretation stands in need of correction. Thus, when the author was confronted with the following sentences he was induced to seek additional information in order to resolve the conflict of these data with the prevailing ethnological construction of a Wind Soul which stands unchanged within the individual, producing good or bad conduct depending on its own character:

> Then (at boyhood) there is a really good one standing within but nevertheless they misbehave. (HB)
> When our thinking, the one that stands within us, becomes tired, this Little Wind sends others from there (the four cardinal directions) so that our thinking is strong, the one standing within us is strong. It takes it out (i.e., the one that became tired). (CAB)

The terms concorded fall into several categories. The foremost in terms of the number of entries are those terms directly referring to Winds including terms translated as Wind's Child, Little Winds, the Wind within one, Wind People, Holy Wind and so forth. The majority of these data have been incorporated into the body of this paper in the form of the translated statements of informants and in the appendix in their original Navajo language form. Another category includes various Navajo terms commonly used by informants in expressing beliefs related to theological and cosmological concepts, such as the terms for the Holy Ones, the underworlds, Dawn, and Child of Darkness. Many of these data have also been incorporated into the present book. A third category of concorded terms consists of those found to be commonly used by informants and in mythological texts in describing human behavior, Navajo terms for describing "the way one is," "one who has faults," "one who lacks faults," "one who is quick-tempered" and the like. Only a small part of these data have been presented here where they form the basis for the discussion of personality attributes found in the chapter dealing with principles of life and behavior.

Finally, what might at first appear as a problem in translation stems from the Navajo conception that Wind in its totality is comprised of many different Winds. Sometimes the focus is on the fact of unity in which case it is then spoken of and translated in singular form while at other times the plural form is used. Unless the Navajo conception is considered, that there is one Wind comprised of its many aspects, the frequent shift from the singular to the plural will seem to be an inconsistency. This should become clearer as the Navajo point of view comes to be appreciated in the following chapters.

Acknowledgments

Primary credit for the ideas set for in this book must be given to ten Navajo elders who shared with me some part of their knowledge about Navajo ethnopsychology. My role, ideally, has been to faithfully report and interpret their thoughts to a new audience. Some of these men are now gone. All of them must remain unnamed in order to respect expressed, or even unexpressed, desires for confidentiality.

The task of comprehending the elders' point of view would have been impossible without the assistance of young bilingual Navajos who worked with me as interpreters, transcribers, and translators. I particularly recall and appreciate the efforts of John T. Begay, Irene Stewart, Wilson Shorty, Babette Holliday, Lorenzo Isaac, and Kee Jackson. Library research was facilitated by Katharine Bartlett of the Museum of Northern Arizona in Flagstaff who guided me through the Museum Library's collection of Father Berard Haile's manuscripts and other pertinent studies of Navajo thought.

This book grew out of a Ph.D. dissertation in anthropology at the University of Hawaii. Professor Oswald Werner of Northwestern University kindly included me in the Northwestern Field School in Anthropology and Linguistics in the summer of 1969 and thereafter has been, as friend and mentor, a rare source of personal and intellectual support. I am also indebted to Professor Stephen T. Boggs of the Department of Anthropology, University of Hawaii, who stayed by me through the difficult dissertation-writing years; and, to the National Institute of Mental Health for their support of my fieldwork under an Individual Research Fellowship Grant (#1-FO1-MH50474).

David M. Brugge, anthropologist and friend, critically read the initial draft of the book manuscript and provided me with a detailed and thoughtful commentary which materially strengthened the present work. The editorial staff of the Press prompted and guided the final refinements; I owe special thanks to Marshall Townsend and Mildred S. Matthews for their help in this regard.

My wife, Grace, shared with those cited above in virtually all aspects of this work as sometimes informant, interpreter, translator, friend, and constant supporter.

Responsibility for this, the final product, is solely my own.

J. K. McN.

NÍLCH'I: A NOTE ON TRANSLATIONS

In order to be consistent with established usage, the term *nílch'i* has been translated in this book as "wind" although this clearly does not adequately convey the sense of the Navajo word. *Nílch'i* refers to the air or atmosphere in its entirety, including such air when in motion, conceived as having a holy quality and powers that are not acknowledged in Western culture. In order to emphasize the latter aspect of the Navajo concept, the phrase Holy Wind has sometimes been used although Spirit or Holy Spirit could perhaps as well be used. Holy Wind Spirit was suggested by Professor Oswald Werner at the 1972 Pecos Conference in Flagstaff, Arizona.

Since the traditional Navajo do not conceive of the Wind within one as being immutable or discrete from that existing everywhere, the usual translation of *nílch'i hwii'sizíinii* as the "in-standing" or "in-dwelling Wind Soul" should be discarded. "The Wind within one" should adequately serve in its stead without implying that it is fixed there for life.

WIND
CONCEPTS

Interpretations and Contradictions

Nı́łch'i, meaning Wind, Air, or Atmosphere, as conceived by the Navajo, is endowed with powers that are not acknowledged in Western culture. Suffusing all of nature, Holy Wind gives life, thought, speech, and the power of motion to all living things and serves as the means of communication between all elements of the living world. As such, it is central to Navajo philosophy and world view. This study concerns *nı́łch'i* as it relates to human behavior; the central thesis is that by this concept the Navajo Soul is linked to the immanent powers of the universe.

While the extent to which the Wind concept pervades virtually all aspects of Navajo ideology has long been intimated in published discussions of Navajo cosmology, theology, mythology, and psychology, there has been lacking a clear understanding of the Navajo view of Wind and of its functions in the dynamics of the Navajo relationship to his world (for earlier interpretations of the Navajo Wind concept, see especially Haile 1943; Reichard 1970 [1950]:50–79; Wyman 1962:36–41; and, Wyman et al. 1942:11–49). Witherspoon's (1977) work has given explicit recognition to the central role of Wind in the

Navajo universe and has resolved some of the contradictions in earlier interpretations of the Wind concept. This book is addressed to the task of further clarifying this important Navajo philosophical concept, particularly as it is applied in explanations of human thought and behavior.

Some of the contradictions in our understanding of the Wind concept have existed between ethnographic data and ethnological interpretations of those data. The literature does not generally acknowledge the primary role of Wind in the Navajo universe. Yet Frank Goldtooth gave an account of the creation story in which Supreme Sacred Wind appeared as the Supreme Creator of this world (Fishler 1953:9–11); Hostiin Klah acknowledged that after the present world was created only First Man, First Woman, "Yolgi Asdzaan" (White Bead Woman or Changing Woman), and Winds had god-like powers (Klah 1942:95); and, Haile noted a tradition which assigns to Wind together with Wind Deer a primary role in the creation of the universe (Haile 1943:81).

Other contradictions have existed between differing interpretations of related Navajo concepts and beliefs, as in conflicting views of Navajo psychology. Father Berard Haile found in Navajo psychology a belief that every person has a Wind Soul within him that is autonomous with respect to the person, entering at birth, completely controlling the thought and behavior of the individual throughout his life, and then departing at death (Haile 1943:76–83). So impressed was Haile by this belief, as he understood it, that he concluded that there is no room in the Navajo conception of man for individual volition, conscience, morality, merit, reward, accountability, or punishment (Haile 1951:169). On the other hand, Gladys Reichard failed to detect in Navajo psychology such an autonomous Wind Soul. She recognized, to be sure, that the Navajo Wind deity is conceived to furnish the "breath of life" to the individual, but she also found the belief that throughout his lifetime the individual can ritually inhale the "breath power" of helpful supernaturals and exorcise the "breath poison" of harmful powers (Reichard 1943:355–356; 1970 [1950]: 33–34). Furthermore, in her interpretation, man is conceived to be endowed with awareness, volition, and the capacity to control his own destiny with the ritually-secured assistance of supernatural powers (Reichard 1943:357; 1970 [1950]: 34–35).

Luckert's interpretation of Navajo thought also casts some doubt on Haile's attribution of the soul concept to the Navajo, arguing that a holistic view of man dominates Navajo ideology, man's mental faculties not being abstracted from his bodily appearance (Luckert

1975:152). Luckert relates this holistic view of man to the Navajo conception of "prehuman flux," a conception which expresses human kinship with all living beings, each of which has a person-like essence that is capable of interchanging appearances with other living beings. While recognizing that there are in Navajo thinking about man "traces" of a body-soul dualistic theory — or possibly even a pluralistic theory attributing several temporary souls to a given body — Luckert suggests that Father Berard's own cultural background and position may have colored his more valid insights into Navajo thought.

> Writing for the benefit of fellow Christians, Father Berard has studied the Navajo view of man from the perspective of a Hellenic-Christian body-soul dualism.... But after all has been said concerning the dominant Navajo "soul concept," Father Berard comes down to a simple study of "inner forms" [author's note: the person-like essences common to all life]. To please Western minds and church-supported publishers it eventually may be significant to learn that these inner forms might have souls; but for understanding traditional thought, I believe, Father Berard's specific observations concerning inner forms are much more important (Luckert 1975:161).

Nevertheless, Haile's attribution to the Navajo of a belief in a Wind Soul continues to dominate interpretations of Navajo psychology. Witherspoon accepts Haile's view that a Wind Soul is thought to be dispatched into the individual at birth as the source of the individual's life, breath, thought and action, although he departs from Haile in arguing that while the Wind Soul is thought by the Navajo to give the individual the capacity for thought and action, it does not control these functions. With Reichard, on this particular issue, he holds that the Navajo view is that it is *man* who thinks (Witherspoon 1977:29–31, 41–44).

The above-mentioned interpretations of Navajo psychology offer, in effect, highly divergent views of the nature of man, all of which are attributed to the Navajo. The ethnographic data to be presented here will, it is believed, help towards resolving some of these differences, most of which can be traced to misinterpretations of the Navajo concept of Wind. The data constitute a clear challenge to existing constructions of not only the Navajo concept of Wind but also to related theories and beliefs concerning relationships between man and the deities, and the nature and sources of morality. Preliminary evidence for this challenge may be found in the existing literature in the form of the recorded statement of the informant whom Haile considered as being his best authority on the Wind Soul, a statement which is not explicable in terms of current ethnological understanding of the Wind or Air concept. The informant indicated that Dawn Woman determines which Wind Soul shall enter the child to be born and that these Wind Souls report back to her on the lives of the persons controlled by them: "If the in-standing Wind reports untoward actions, like adultery, theft, and the like, these may be punished in the lifetime of the person" (Haile 1943:82, 87).

The above statement stands as an enigma for two reasons. First, it indicates that the individual's Wind Soul or in-standing Wind somehow reports to a deity about the individual's behavior during the course of the individual's life; and second, it suggests that supernatural punishment may follow socially or supernaturally disapproved behavior. Haile could not account for the statement, for his construction of the Wind Soul allowed only for its entrance at birth, its departure at death, and its complete governance of life and behavior in between, with no provision for its contact during the individual's life with Dawn Woman or any other supernatural agent; and, despite his informant's singular statement about punishment, Haile remained convinced that the thought of punishment does not enter into Navajo ideology at all (Haile 1943:87). Haile, of course, does not stand alone in these respects. Existing understandings of the Wind Soul concept do not postulate a reporting to supernatural beings during the individual's life; the prevailing opinion of ethnologists is that Navajo deities are not moral legislators or moral authorities in any sense (e.g., Kluckhohn 1949:368; Ladd 1957:217, 262; Aberle 1966:50).

The reconstructed Wind concept to be presented herein will satisfactorily account for the statement made by Haile's informant as well as account for the new ethnographic data which form the basis for this study. The revised model of the Wind concept will offer a view of Navajo psychology that is less ego-centered than existing views, arguing that the Navajo conceive of thought and behavior as being strongly externally determined rather than originating primarily within the individual. The deities will be seen to have primary roles in governing human thought and behavior, and man will be viewed as participating directly in supernatural powers rather than as identifying with them indirectly through symbolic processes. Finally, a view of Navajo morality will be presented in which the Holy People, by means of Wind, have a direct role in shaping and enforcing moral behavior. The net effect of this reconstruction will be to suggest that the Navajo traditionally conceive of the individual's behavioral and moral characteristics as being manifestations of similar characteristics existing in the powers of the universe, rather than as expressions of a differentiated Wind Soul dwelling within.

THEORY AND MYTH

The ethnological and ethnographic difficulties cited above are resolvable only by examining the total Navajo theoretical context from which conceptions of Wind, of man, of deity, and of morality derive their meanings. This theoretical context is founded in and structured around the sequence of events related in the Navajo creation story, the sacred oral traditions which account for the beginnings of the Navajo universe and the creation of life. The outline of this creation story is well described in existing recorded versions of Navajo mythology, as summarized by Spencer:

> In content the general origin myth includes events in the lower worlds, the emergence to the present world, the creation of people and objects in the present world, the birth and childhood of the war gods, their journey to the sun, their exploits in ridding the world of monsters, and an account of clan origins. This myth deals with the beginnings of things: the preparation of the physical world, the creation of its inhabitants, and the place of the Navaho in this world. It seems to be treated as the most central and most sacred of the stories in Navaho folklore (Spencer 1947:12).

The general origin myth may be told as a preface to one of the chantway myths of the Navajo healing ceremonials which branch off from it at various points (Spencer 1947:12; Wyman 1962:31–32). Each such chantway myth is distinctive in relating the origins of a particular ceremonial, but there is a common theme underlying most of them, as described by Spencer:

> Navaho ceremonialism centers around curing. The chant origin myths for the individual ceremonies follow a generalized pattern. They recount the adventures of a Navaho who has become separated from his people, how he has a curing ceremony performed over him by the gods, and finally how this person who was the patient in the divine performance returns and teaches the ceremony to his people. These myths are full of ceremonial details that may serve as a guide to the present-day conduct of the ceremony (Spencer 1947:12).

While this book is not generally concerned with these chantway myths, there are several instances in which they do contribute theoretical context for concepts under investigation here. For example, versions of the origin myths of the Navajo Windway and Chiricahua Windway ceremonials provide insights into the Navajo Wind concept. Secondly, some of the chantway myths recount portions of the general origin myth thereby providing additional versions of the events involved in Navajo ethnohistory.

Standing apart from the chantway ceremonials and their associated myths is the rite and myth of Blessingway which is also a rich source of data about Navajo world view. The Blessingway rite is primarily used to invoke positive blessings and to protect from misfortune rather than to cure illness, remove injury, or to restore good health or favorable conditions (Wyman and Kluckhohn 1938:18; Wyman 1970: 409). The myth consists essentially of the post-emergence events of the origin myth with special emphasis on the creation of the present world, the birth and blessings of Changing Woman, the creation of the Navajo, the origin of clans, and the origin of the Blessingway rite (Wyman 1970:41). Blessingway is often considered to hold a central or controlling position in the Navajo religious system, giving unity to the whole and providing themes for many of the acts and procedures in the chantway ceremonies (Wyman 1970:5; Haile 1938:652; Brugge 1963:25).

The Navajo origin myth, then, including segments of those chantway and rite origin myths which relate events of the origin myth, and the Windway myths which provide insight into the role of Wind in Navajo religious ideology, are the conceptual foundations of traditional Navajo psychological thought. The methods of this investigation were designed to explore these foundations as well as the philosophical system constructed on them.

HOLY WIND
BEFORE EMERGENCE

In setting forth conceptions of the nature of Wind and sanctions for their beliefs about its role in human life and behavior, bearers of the Navajo oral traditions characteristically recite appropriate passages of the creation story. This myth accounts for the beginnings of existence, the birth or creation of various Peoples in worlds that are conceived to have existed beneath Earth's surface, the emergence of these Peoples through those worlds to the surface of the Earth, and the subsequent creation of the present world on Earth's surface and of its specific inhabitants. Beliefs concerning the attributes of Wind and the nature of its relationships with other living beings are to be found in accounts of the underworlds. Sources may be found there for the conceptions that Wind has existed as a holy being from near the beginnings of the Navajo universe, being endowed with the power to give life and movement to other beings and possessed of knowledge which it conveyed to the Holy People. Review of parts of these myths will help to clarify the significance and place of Wind in Navajo ideology.

MISTS OF LIGHT

Many versions of creation begin with descriptions of light which "misted up" from the horizons of the otherwise darkened underworlds. These mists of light, dawn in the east, sky blue in the south, evening twilight in the west and darkness in the north, arose from the aforementioned cardinal directions which were also marked by four mountains. The mists are said to have been the means of breath of the mountains associated with them, and within each of them, in turn, was an inner form "just like a real breathing human" (Haile n.d.*b*:2; see also a variant version in Haile 1930:50). In this way the mists of light and the mountains of the cardinal directions are believed to have been living, breathing phenomena.

SOURCE OF LIFE

It is from the cardinal points so conceived that Winds came to the inhabitants of the underworlds to give life and power to them, as in the following account in which First Man and First Woman, who had been produced by Earth, were given strength. In this version, a single mist or cloud became the source of the Winds as well as of the diurnal cycle of light phenomena:

> While they were waiting for strength they saw a Cloud of Light in the east which kept rising and falling.... While they watched, it turned black, and from that blackness they saw the Black Wind coming. Then the Cloud of Light turned blue and they saw the Blue Wind coming to them, then it turned yellow and the Yellow Wind appeared, and then it turned white and the White Wind came. Finally the light showed all colors and the Many Colored Wind came.... This Cloud of Light also created the Rainbow of the Earth and as the light changes it creates *hayołkááł*, the White Early Dawn; *nahodeetl'izh*, the Blue Sky of noon and also the blue that comes after the dawn; *nahootsoi*, the Yellow of Sunset; and *chahałheeł*, the Dark of Night. These were also made for the people of the Earth, and each of these is a holy time of the day from which comes certain powers (Haile 1933*b*:97–98).

The life-giving qualities of the Winds are indicated in the subsequent passage:

> When the Winds appeared and entered life they passed through the bodies of men and creatures and made the lines on the fingers, toes and heads of human beings, and on the bodies of the

different animals. The Wind has given men and creatures strength ever since, for at the beginning they were shrunken and flabby until it inflated them, and the Wind was creation's first food, and put motion and change into nature giving life to everything, even to the mountains and water (Haile 1933*b*:97–98).

By one account, Wind created by the mists of light not only gave life to all living things but, as Supreme Sacred Wind, became the Supreme Creator of the Navajo universe:

> The mists came together and laid on top of each other, like intercourse, and Supreme Sacred Wind was created.... Supreme Sacred Wind lived in light and black clouds or mists in space (Fishler 1953:9).

In this version, Supreme Sacred Wind, a being having the form of a person and knowing all that happens, created First Man, First Woman, and such Holy People as Talking God, Calling God, Coyote, and Black God. These Holy People, and the others he created, derived their special powers from him: "After the Supreme Sacred Wind delegated His powers over to the gods, down below, He did not have power over their powers, only in part" (Fishler 1953:9–28).

SOURCE OF THOUGHT

Whether conceived of as a Supreme Creator or not, Wind made life possible in the underworlds not only by providing a means by which breathing could occur but also by providing guidance and protection to those who were created or born there. This conception is elaborated upon in an account which is quoted at length below in view of its unusually extensive description of the role of Wind as a guide or mentor. What is presented as a single narrative is actually a compilation of myth fragments elicited from the informant (JT) during several different interviews. As is customary, this history recounts the beginnings of the Earth and of existence, again associating Wind with phenomena of light:

> Wind existed first, as a person, and when the Earth began its existence Wind took care of it.
> We started existing where Darknesses, lying on one another, occurred. Here, the one that had lain on top became Dawn, whitening across. What used to be lying on one another back then, this is Wind. It (Wind) was Darkness. That is why when Darkness

settles over you at night it breezes beautifully. It is this, it is a person, they say. From there when it dawns, when it dawns beautifully becoming white-streaked through the Dawn, it usually breezes. Wind exists beautifully, they say. Back there in the underworlds, this was a person it seems.[1] (JT)

The peoples of the underworlds migrated from place to place, initially lacking in plans or a sense of direction:

In this way they lived back then and from there they moved to the place called Navajo Land. From there it is called One Word, it probably being spoken according to one word. There they went around like sheep. Like sheep, they did not talk. Their eyes governed their actions—if they are going to go *this* way, *that* way they run! Then *this* way! That is the way it was. There was no language, so they merely looked at one another. What would be used (the words that would be used in the future) to talk to each other, there were none. To go over there (to direct one another) they said, "whoo, whoo," and they understood very well. In that way it was called Word One back then. From then they were Holy People, all four-legged animals being people. First Man and First Woman led them.

First Man, First Woman, Talking God, Calling God, these Holy People lived in this way.... "I will see for you," he (Wind) said. So, in this way Wind was obtained. Wind existed first and they encountered it as a person. Then, it seems, he continued: "Things will be known by me. With you it is not known where you will go. You do not know!" he said. "I know!" he said. "I know all about everything. I know about what is in this Earth and what is on it," he said. "I am Wind!" In this way back then he told about himself. There he became that which gives life. "Thank you, you accepted us," they said.

In this way, according to the way of the two lying on one another, they started off. That which was Darkness and also that which was Dawn became Winds. The one that was called in that way (Darkness?) will be called Dark Wind. When blueness appears at dawn, that will be called Blue Wind.

What was thinking, what was Wind, became words (language). "I will inform you," he said. "How is he going to tell us? He is Wind so how will it be?" "That will be known among ourselves—now I will just tell you!" he said again. Four times this happened, but he did not tell them. He did not say, "I will tell you" (Wind is here refusing to tell the people of the means by which he will inform them of things).

So they went forth from there. Yonder is what will be called "the Place of Separation." Through here a river is flowing. There, very awesome red mountains are located. The land is the same—spreading out beneath the mountains there it is red, too. The river, also, is reddish as it flows. "It is very beautiful here. We will live here from now on," it was said. Already then it (Wind) was in use: "You will move to here!" it was said to them through here—here, it seems, through the earfold where it cannot be seen. When we poke our fingers or stick something in here we touch it and are aware of it. It (Wind) is in here. From there it speaks to them. "Settle right here," is was said to them. "Right here!"[2] (JT)

Here, the informant has related how Wind told things to the people, that is, through a corner of the ear which could not be seen. This, as was mentioned above, is what Wind had refused to tell the people themselves—*how* he would speak to them. The narrative continues:

"It's really true what he said!" (they thought). From that time, whatever Wind spoke, it began happening in that way. Here they settled and having settled there suddenly it was spoken again from here (inside the ear): "You will make a leader," it was said to them. "The leader will be foremost among you. You will live under him, he standing for you. He will be your continuous leader and in that way you will live orderly," it was said to them.

Some women are very feared. These women are strong leaders, they act strongly, they speak out. There was this kind, called Woman Leader. "What will she say about what was said to us from here (in the ear)?" (they said). "Come here, listen!" they said to her, and they told her about it: "I was told that back there at the place called Darkness Crosses we came upon Wind Person and there he planned for us saying, 'Only according to my way will things be.' This is the situation now," it was said to her. So then: "That's right, it is true my children, they say that it's true. It was spoken to us like that, and within us it [Wind] is placed and to us it speaks. It (he) is our thinking."

So for that reason, things will happen according to his (Wind's) will. From that time what is called "leadership was formed" came into being: "What is called leadership will be placed; what is called speaking will be placed. Now it exists. Perhaps you know how to provide leadership? Perhaps you know words which you will use to make speeches? again it was said. "Yes, we know!" "Alright, now it will be!" Way back there is when leadership was formed.

Here, leadership was again placed. The words by means of which speeches will be made and the words by means of which threats will be spoken were placed. From here (in his ear) he (Wind) was saying that by his will "You will proceed in this way so as not to make mistakes—not to proceed just according to your own mind, just as you want to do." They followed in this way. In this way leadership was formed there, Wind telling the one who is Talking God about it through here (his earfold).[3] (JT)

To review and interpret this account, the various peoples went around aimlessly like sheep, lacking language and without plans, until they came upon Wind in the form of a person who knew all and who told them that henceforth he would speak to them (through the corners of their ears). Wind then gave leadership to them and the words by which they would exercise this, the knowledge and the means to lead themselves. Even then, however, Wind gave them only a restricted governance over their lives so that a leader would not be able to do anything that he wanted to, "just according to one's mind." Rather, Wind made available the means of speaking particular words, including the threatening words needed by a leader.

The actual exercise of leadership in the underworlds, as distinguished from its establishment by Wind, was by chiefs who were appointed in one way or another to perform such functions as teaching the people how to farm and calling them together each day in order to tell them what to do (for the roles of chiefs, see the review of mythological accounts of chiefs and their roles in Spencer 1947:70–81). Even so, the conception by native historians of a continuing influence by Wind over these chiefs is evident. For example, informant JT related that Wind told the son-in-law of Woman Leader to get up and go out on a platform each day and tell the others what to do. Similarly, informant JD while recognizing that First Man and First Woman were leaders of many activities in the underworlds said that Wind advised them what they should do:

The way we are telling things to each other, back then it (Wind) in the same way told them, "You should do this, you (two) should do this," being told thusly. So it is true. Back then it (Wind) told them. They used to live by it.[4] (JT)

The guidance and sustenance provided by Wind to leaders in the underworlds is the prototype of Wind's relationship to the Holy People during the course of their emergence to Earth's surface and of its subsequent relationship to human beings, the Earth Surface People in the world created on Earth's surface following the emergence from the underworlds:

Dark Wind, Blue Wind, Yellow Wind, White Wind, Glossy Wind, we will speak in accordance with their will—it happened (was said) like this. So, accordingly, one who speaks in our behalf has been present alongside us from back then. These same Winds speak for us and spoke for our late ancestors. Our leaders who speak for us held on to the ones that guide us. So back there they (Winds) told us that we live in accordance with their wishes.[5] (JT)

By one account, it is even due to Wind's precedent that Earth Surface People later assumed responsibility for each other: "Now Winds will take care of us from the beginning of our lives. In accordance with that we will take care of each other from now on."[6] (JT)

Prior to elaborating upon the Navajo conception of Wind as a source of support and guidance to present-day human beings, the structure and dynamics of this present world on Earth's surface must be understood from the traditional Navajo point of view. These matters are addressed in the next chapter.

Attention has been directed to Navajo conceptions of the origins, attributes, and roles of Winds in the underworlds as revealed in versions of origin and chantway myths. Many accounts of creation commence with the misting upwards of light of various colors in the cardinal directions of the underworlds, these light mists being the loci of the Winds. Winds are said to have given the means of breath and life to the Peoples of the underworlds and to have provided them with guidance and leadership by speaking into their ears. Subsequent chapters will reflect Navajo beliefs about the emergence of these Winds along with other Holy People onto Earth's surface and their roles in the lives of the Peoples and other living beings of the present world.

The
PRESENT
WORLD

The nature of the world created on Earth's surface, according to Navajo tradition, is recounted in published versions of the Navajo creation story (see especially Haile 1930 or Wyman 1970) and will not be described here in great detail. What is relevant to the present purpose is the extent to which life, thought, and the means of communication are conceived to suffuse this world. This conception provides the foundation for a basic tenet in Navajo psychology which is that elements of the world are equipped to provide guidance and instruction, by means of Wind, to Earth Surface People. This chapter will examine the Navajo view of this world as it provides a foundation for traditional Navajo psychology.

EMERGENCE OF WIND

For Wind to continue to function as the means of life and thought for the inhabitants of the world on Earth's surface, as it had done in the underworlds, would necessarily require that it emerge from the underworlds along with the other Holy People. This conception is, in fact, expressed by informant BY:

> At the place of emergence are four layers (worlds). They emerged with it (Wind) from there—the Holy People came out through twelve big reeds connected together. They came up from there with ceremonials. Wind exists from there, from way back then. It did not form recently. (BY)

In another account, by informant CAB, it is Earth Woman who placed Wind in the cardinal directions of the present world for people to live by. This account merits careful attention not only for its concept of the process by which Wind was placed on Earth's surface but even more for its clarification of the relationships between Wind and the life and behavior of Earth Surface People. One may recall that in the underworlds it was as two Winds lying on one another that Wind gave life and guidance to the Peoples existing there (see pp. 9–10). It is Wind so conceived that also came to provide life and guidance in this world. As in the underworlds, Wind is closely associated with "word" or "language":

> Within the one called Earth Mother two Winds formed, one lying on top of the other. These were put up here for us.
> The Earth faces toward the east, her feet being placed over there where the Sun goes down. From there she spoke her foremost word. When she spoke they were embarrassed: "From now on you will urinate on me and defecate on me and do whatever to me and throw bad things on me. And when you die you will go back in the Earth. You will not go elsewhere," she said.
> "This placed within me by which I spoke will not die—the one lived by, these lying on one another," she said. "This first one placed within me, that will be holy, that will move us, we will live according to it from now on," she said. "And the one we will rest by will also be put on you." In this way it happened; she put her hands towards the east on top of her head, reached out and from there put her hand on where our eyebrows are. The nap of our eyebrows formed here. "By means of this, sleep and rest will be," so it happened (was said). Then to the same place she put her hand out again. From where her fingers met, where our eyebrows are, she ran her finger to here, to where the tip of our nose is. "This will be your thinking, this you will think by," it was said to us.*

---

*This sentence reflects the traditional Navajo conception that the nose is one seat of thought.

"What was put inside Earth will exist over there in the east. It will be called Word One. On this side, to the south, what was *bik'eh hózhǫ* will be Word Two, she said. "After that, two will be added to you placed in between; in the west will be Word Three; in the north (will be Word Four). So four leading words will be placed," it was said. This Word One is very holy, it is female. Following is a male one, again a female one, again a male one, making four altogether.[7] (CAB)

By this account, then, the two "winds lying on one another" from within the Earth by which she spoke to the people were placed on Earth's surface for Earth Surface People. The first one, placed in the east, is very holy, is female, and it gives direction to life. Word Two in the south is *bik'eh hózhǫ* and it is male, being the other of the two "Winds lying on one another" by which Earth spoke.[†] Another female Word was added in the west and another male one in the north. These four Words which were put up in the four directions are conceived to be the Winds by which man is given direction of his life, movement, thinking, and action to carry out plans. These are the same as "the wind standing within us" which enters in the process of reproduction:

It is the same. As we keep reproducing, in that way it is put inside of us. The Words that were spoken are holy, and it is holy on this side (within us), but it is the same. This male Word (in the south) is our gait (or power of movement) — this same Wind is our gait by which we walk. The next one, Word Three, is our thinking (by means of which) we will think for ourselves, plan for ourselves, talk for ourselves. Word Four is when we go by our plans. It is that way.

So Wind became our power of movement and the same one stood within us, moving supernaturally. Next, another just like it, that *bik'eh hózhǫ*, was placed on it, the two lying on one another, these becoming our Words. Then, "From there the one that will move us will exist," happened (was said).[8] (CAB)

While these Winds placed in the cardinal directions enter within people as "the one standing within us," other Winds formed on Earth's surface which could also influence human life and behavior: Two Winds emerged from the Earth, two came from the water, and

---

[†]The meaning of *bik'eh hózhǫ* in this context is uncertain. A literal translation of the phrase might be "according to it there is beauty around one." For discussion of this concept see Witherspoon (1977:23–25).

another two came from the clouds; when these met, six Winds were formed above and six below. We live between these (according to this view) all of which affect us and some of which cause difficulties and sickness:

> We live between them—all human beings. All of them affect us. This Revolving Wind is not very good, and the one called Coiled Wind is not good. This Striped Wind and again four (i.e., another four are not good). These cause different kinds of things to happen. On that side Earth revolves (and) up above Sky revolves, like this (here, the informant indicated the manner of their movement by gestures, Earth and sky revolving circularly but in opposite directions to one another). We live between them. From this, problems increase. In this way we were placed, all human beings. On both sides (Earth's and Sky's) bad things happen.[9] (CAB)

In this way, harmful or problem-causing Winds as well as beneficent ones are conceived to have come into existence on Earth's surface to influence life and behavior.

UNITY OF WIND

What is necessary to stress, in view of the naming of twelve Winds existing on Earth's surface is that, as in the underworlds, Wind is conceived of as a single phenomenon, a deity formed as it were of component Winds which exist all about and within the living things of the world. As informant GES expressed it, "There is only one Wind but it has five names, Dark Wind, Blue Wind, Yellow Wind, White Wind, Glossy Wind, Wind's child (naming, in fact, six instead of five).[10] Other informants, while accepting the basic premise that there is only one Wind, say that it has twelve names. Navajo naming of a particular aspect of Wind does not thereby differentiate it as a kind of Wind having no relationship to the whole of which it is a part, just as our naming of a sea does not imply that the waters referred to are distinct from the great body of water encompassing the whole Earth.

It is difficult, at least initially, to grasp the Navajo conception of a unitary Wind which bears different names and has diverse characteristics. In order to clarify this concept, attention must be paid to the process of naming that results in these numerous appellations. A reference in a version of the Chiricahua Windway myth to Wavy

Backed Wind exemplifies this process, for there Wavy Backed Wind does not refer to a different kind of Wind but rather to the *appearance* of the Winds of the cardinal directions, Dark Wind, Blue Wind, White Wind, and Yellow Wind, as they travel to a ceremonial performance. Haile noted, "The 'wavy back' is suggested by the dust caused by the winds coming to the performance on their hoops" (Haile 1932*b*:129). If this process were generalized, other names would be generated for Wind depending on its appearance in other situations.

Consistent with the above is informant JD's statement that the different names applied to Wind in the cardinal directions are in accordance with the principle that for a Navajo ceremonial to be complete all of the cardinal directions must be named, and that the naming of Wind in a given ceremonial context is in terms of the colors assigned to the cardinal directions in the ideology and symbolism of that particular ceremonial. In JD's example of the Chiricahua Windway ceremonial, Wind is given four names, Dark Wind in the east, Blue Wind in the south, White Wind in the west, and Yellow Wind in the north in line with the color symbolism of that ceremonial, but these names all have a common referent. They "all come back together."

It appears that Wind is assigned multiple names in accordance with such criteria as the color symbolism of the direction of its origin (as in the example given by JD, cited above); its locus (e.g., the Wind standing within one); its size (e.g., Little Wind); its appearance (e.g., Wavy Backed Wind); its character or possible effects (e.g., harmful Wind); and, its direction of rotation (e.g., Wind turning sunwise). Nevertheless, there is only one Wind in the Navajo view, conceived to exist in these different directions and loci and to have various appearances, sizes, effects, and directions of rotation in different situations and at different times.

INNER FORMS OF THE CARDINAL DIRECTIONS

It may be recalled that in the underworlds Wind came to the Peoples living there from the mists of light existing in the cardinal directions and that these mists also contained inner forms likened to human forms which were the breathing means of the mountains situated in the four directions. This cosmological arrangement is essentially replicated in the present world.

What had been the mists of light in the underworlds were, by some accounts, changed by First Man and the other planners of this world into the light phenomena as they are now conceived by the

Navajo. For instance, Sandoval related that after the Sun was placed in the Sky, the dark cloud that had appeared in the lower worlds became the Night, the white cloud became the Dawn, and where the blue and yellow clouds had been, there now appeared the Twilight and False Dawn (O'Bryan 1956:15–22). In most versions, new inner forms are placed within the light phenomena of this world. Frank Mitchell's Blessingway account tells that prior to placing Dawn so that it would appear suspended horizontally in the east, Talking God said to it, "I myself will be existing in your interior...." Calling God then placed the one in the west (Evening Twilight) saying that, "I will exist in your interior" (Haile 1930:99). The ones in the south (Sky Blue) and north (Darkness) were similarly placed, and it was said that the ones to exist in their interiors will eventually become known (Wyman 1970:371–372).

Other names also appear in published Navajo mythologies for the inner forms of the cardinal light phenomena, reflecting various sex and generation distinctions. Black Mustache, Haile's informant, named Dawn Woman, Horizontal Blue Girl, Horizontal Yellow Boy, and Darkness Man as the inner forms (Haile 1943:72–73). The Franciscan Fathers listed Dawn Man and Dawn Woman, Azure Man and Azure Woman, Twilight Man and Twilight Woman, and Darkness Man and Darkness Woman (Franciscan Fathers 1910:354–355). Slim Curly spoke of there being two inner forms of the cardinal directions, the east-south-west semicircle being male and the west-north-east semicircle being female (Haile 1932a:49–51). Haile therefore concluded that although there may be differences of opinion concerning the sex of these persons it is generally recognized that the cardinal points have inner forms (Haile 1943:71).

SACRED MOUNTAINS

Similar, if not the same, beings as those in the phenomena of light are conceived to have been placed within the mountains created in the cardinal directions of the present world. In making the mountains of the east, south, west and north, soil which had been brought up from the principal mountains of the underworlds was mixed with white shell, turquoise, abalone, and jet, respectively; or the mountains and their inner forms were decorated with these jewels along with other adornments. According to Frank Mitchell's detailed account, the planners at the rim of the place of emergence decided that "the one to stand for them" (the mountains' inner forms) must be "absolutely faultless" (*ts'ídá ba'ádinii*), one who "does not think two ways" (Haile 1930:57). They then decided that some beings patterned after Talking God and Calling God should be especially made for this purpose from the materials used in decorating the mountains, so White Shell Talking God, Turquoise Calling God, Abalone Talking God, and Jet Talking God were created to stand within the mountains. Gobernador Knob was also made and placed upon Earth's heart, and Huerfano Mountain was made and set upon Earth's lungs. First Man said that the ones to live within them would come into existence later. By these means, the principal mountains were given "those that stand within them" and it is said that they possess a means of breathing and of speaking to each other so that they are really alive (Haile 1930:28–57; 480–481).

The names given by informants to the inner forms of the sacred mountains are indicative of associations between them and the inner forms of the phenomena of light. While the names of the mountains' inner forms vary from one account to another, they most consistently encode distinctions between the phenomena of light of the four directions or between the kinds of jewels associated with the mountains of the east, south, west, and north, respectively. White Shell Talking God, White Shell Boy, and Dawn Boy, for instance, all seem to be identified with the Holy Person who is the inner form of the sacred mountain of the east, just as Abalone Talking God, Abalone Boy, and Twilight Boy are identified with the inner form of the sacred mountain of the west. While these names are suggestive of conceptual relationships between these inner forms and the Talking God and Calling God inner forms of the phenomena of light, considerable ambiguity remains as to precisely how these relationships are viewed by the Navajo. In one view, Talking God "in the form of White Shell Talking God" and Calling God "in the form of Turquoise Calling God" were placed in the sacred mountains of the east (Wyman 1970:495–507). It seems that although Talking God and Calling God appear in some legends as the inner forms of Dawn and Evening Twilight respectively, their "homes" are conceived to be on the summits of Blanca Peak and San Francisco Peak (for Haile's discussion of this point, see Haile 1951:40, 294).

THE MEANS OF KNOWING THINGS

The inner forms of the phenomena of light and mountains associated with the cardinal directions are conceived to have been endowed with powers of great significance for the human life to be subsequently created on Earth's surface. The placement of four Winds in these same cardinal locations was not fortuitous, for these Winds were to be the means by which the inner forms would communicate with others and know what is happening on Earth's surface:

> Then the Winds were stationed at the horizon to guard the earth, and at the four sacred mountains in the east, south, west, and north, to act as messengers for the *Haashch'ééłti'í* and *Haashch'éoghaan* — Talking Gods and House Gods — who had their abodes on them (Curtis 1907:89–93).*

By other accounts, while Talking and Calling Gods of the mountains are said to have the means of supernatural travel to enable them to know and to direct things, Wind's Child directs such travels by speaking to them through the ear (Wyman 1970:495–497). Winds are also said to have been placed at the mountains of the east and the west in order to keep the Earth and the Sky informed and to be their means of communication (Wyman 1970:353; Haile 1930:28). In informant CAB's view, the placement of Winds at the mountains accounts for the sacred nature of these mountains:

> They (Winds) stand within the mountains, these (mountains) from then on being, by them, our sacred ones to the end of time. The One that is Holy, the One that made us, then said, "You will live by them." So these (Winds) stand within the mountains, Mount Blanca, Mount Taylor, San Francisco Peaks, Hesperus Peak, Huerfano Mountain, Gobernador Knob.[11] (CAB)

More generally, however, it is the Talking and Calling Gods situated at these mountains who are regarded as being leading chiefs: "Whatever they think will happen accordingly and whatever they speak will so happen." (Wyman 1970:497–498). As possessors of the means of supernatural travel or with the aid of Messenger Winds they are the "means of knowing things" occurring on Earth's surface (Wyman 1970:497–498). With the creation of Earth Surface People they would assume the role of monitoring, guiding, and directing human life (see the next chapter).

Thus, while the conceptual relationship between the inner forms of the phenomena of light and the inner forms of the mountains of

---

*Curtis' orthography of Navajo terms has here been altered to accord with that used throughout this book. Calling God, rather than House God, is the most common rendition of *Haashch'éoghaan* (Haile 1951:39).

the cardinal directions remains somewhat unclear, it suffices here to take note of the placement of important Holy Ones within natural phenomena of the four cardinal directions as well as the placement of Winds in these four directions by which things are said to be known and by which communication is achieved with others. These features of Navajo ideology provide the foundation for the traditional Navajo theory of life and behavior. The Navajo, as will be seen, look primarily to the Holy Ones of the four directions for their sustenance and guidance.

PROCESS OF CREATION

The creative and life-giving powers attributed to phenomena of the four directions may be seen in accounts of the process by which Wind, and therefore life, was given to other elements of the world on Earth's surface. The version of the process of creation which follows is informative also in its drawing of a parallel between the legendary creation of elements of the natural world and the process of human reproduction, throwing light upon the Navajo conception of the role of Wind in both.

According to informant CM's account, among the Holy People who attended the meeting to create Earth, Sky, Sun, Moon, and various animals were First Man and First Woman, Dawn Man and Dawn Woman, Sky Blue Man and Sky Blue Woman, Twilight Man and Twilight Woman, and Darkness Man and Darkness Woman. Also in attendance were different kinds of Wind People who would give life to the things being created. The above-named inner forms of the cardinal light phenomena placed materials from which the various things would be created in a basket and spread Dawn, Sky Blue, Evening Twilight, and Darkness beneath it and over it.

> Here Dawn Woman and Dawn Man placed a basket and beneath it and on top of it spread the Dawn. Female Sky Blue was spread beneath it (the basket) with Dawn underneath. Dawn Woman, Dawn Man, Sky Blue Woman, Sky Blue Man, Evening Twilight Woman, Evening Twilight Man—these were spread beneath it (in that order). They were spread beneath sheep, horses, hard goods, these being set inside the basket.[12] (CM)

With the inner forms of the cardinal light phenomena lying on top of one another, above and below the basket, other Holy People in attendance sang Blessingway toward it to give life to the creations.

Meanwhile, the inner forms of the cardinal light phenomena had sexual intercourse, and something was formed beneath them:

> Then they sang Blessingway toward it. Not many (songs) were sung—they sang only four (which were) really the ones by which they moved. So these were spread beneath and some were placed on top. Well, Sky Blue Woman (and) Man joined together and here, it seems, they had relations with one another, being covered they "bothered one another" beneath it. Here movement began under where they were spread, some underneath and some male ones on top. Here beneath it, something formed.[13] (CM)

What was formed as the result of the intercourse of the inner forms of the cardinal phenomena was the same thing as the Wind that forms inside of a human embryo when it is conceived. Informant CM referred to his earlier discussion of this process at which time it was explained in this way:

> In having intercourse with a woman, bodily fluids join together and where these are joined a baby is formed. From the man's bodily fluid is the Wind by which he lived and from the woman's is one Wind, too, by which she lived. So there are really two. So there, inside where it (the baby) formed, the one (Wind) existing within it (that) they call *sạ'ạh naagháí,* they call (it) *bik'eh hózhǫ.*[*][14] (CM)

By this same process, but on a cosmic scale if you will, the inner forms of the cardinal phenomena in sexual intercourse brought their Winds together to form the Wind by which that being created would live: "In this way, the one that is Earth's Wind, the one that is Sky's WInd, the one that is Sun's Wind, the one that is Moon's Wind, were made back then." (informant CM)

In many accounts of the creation of Earth and Sky the concepts *sạ'ạh naagháí bik'eh hózhǫ* are identified in various ways with their inner forms rather than with Wind, as in the version cited above (Haile 1930:10, 556; Wyman 1970:347, 481; Klah 1942:63, Haile 1932a:93). The origin of all of these powers within Earth and their working together to bring blessings to things placed on her surface

---

*As with *bik'eh hózhǫ,* the meaning of *sa'ah naagháí* is subject to diverse interpretations, and no translation will be attempted herein. For discussion of this concept see Witherspoon (1977:19–23).

may account for real ambiguity in the Navajo conception, or the ambiguity may reside in our lack of complete data and understanding. In any event, it is clear that inner forms are conceived to have been made for Earth and Sky as well as Winds by which they would be able to breathe and think. Wind's Child was also placed within the resting places for the heads of Earth and Sky, Blanca Peak in the east and San Francisco Peak in the west, respectively, as their means of knowing things (Wyman 1970:353; Haile 1930:28).

Similarly with the Sun and the Moon which had been created. In addition to the Winds that were given them to be their means of life and breath, other Winds became their means of communicating with others (Wyman 1970:391). As with Earth and Sky, "holy beings" were appointed to enter within them as their inner forms (Haile 1951:200, 286–291, 353; Wyman 1970:366, 378).

It is unnecessary here to recapitulate the detail of mythic accounts relating how, in analogous ways, Wind and inner forms were placed within all living things on Earth's surface to be their means of life and breath. It is sufficient to say that such living things as plants, animals, insects and birds conceived to exist in human form, have been given the means of life, movement and speech by Wind, and are thought to be merely attired in the external plant and animal forms by which we recognize them (Wyman 1970:366–368, 400; Haile 1943:67). In addition, Wind's Child placed at the ears of the various living things became their means of hearing, knowing, and communicating with others. By one account, animals are informed even of human thoughts about them: "When we are thinking well of them—horses, cattle, goats, and everything that we live by—they know about it by means of Wind. They know our thinking."[15] (CAB)

CREATION OF HOLY PEOPLE AND EARTH SURFACE PEOPLE

The part placed by Winds in giving life and instruction to the Holy People who were created or born on Earth's surface merits particular attention in that a parallel is sometimes directly drawn by informants between this and the role of Winds in Navajo life. The most complete accounts are available for the birth of Changing Woman who was later instrumental in creating the Navajo. Changing Woman is often referred to as White Bead Woman, although some informants regard these as being two different personages.

It is generally indicated that Changing Woman is the child of a pair of natural phenomena or their inner forms although the identity of this pair varies from one account to another. Thus, this pair have been identified as being Darkness and Dawn (Wheelwright 1949); Dawn Man and Darkness Woman (Franciscan Fathers 1910); Earth Woman and Sky Man (Haile 1930); Earth and Sky (Curtis 1907); Earth Spirit and Sky Spirit (Klah 1942); and, *są'ąh naagháí bik'eh hózhǫ́* (Haile 1932a). As with other beings and phenomena, Winds entered to give Changing Woman life. This is told of by informant CM who stated that four Winds passed through her: Dark Wind entered on her right side from under her feet and came out where her hair spirals out; Blue Wind entered through this hair spiral, passing downward where it came out at the toes of her left foot where it spirals (i.e., the whorls of the skin); similarly, Yellow Wind passed upwards through her body on the left side; and White Wind passed downward through her body on the right side:

> Just when Dark Wind ran upward, black hair was formed. From Blue Wind running downward, these things growing on Earth's surface formed.* That is why here, at the tip of our toes, it spirals—it (Wind) stuck out there. It ran up again, White Wind it was. White hair formed there which turned into grey. (CM)

By one account, a small White Wind was placed in Changing Woman's right ear and a small Dark Wind in her left ear by her parents, Darkness and Dawn. After Changing Woman went to live in the west, these Winds would warn her when her husband, the Sun Carrier, was approaching (Wheelwright 1949:53, 57).

Talking God is said to have been made in a similar manner, having been given life and guidance by Wind. The spirit of life was breathed into him (Franciscan Fathers 1910:383); White Wind was placed within him (Haile 1943b:73); and, Wind's Child was placed along the curves of his ear to direct him by telling him things (Wyman 1970:497). In the same way, various other Holy People were made, with Winds giving them life and being placed at their ears to inform and advise them.

As with the Holy People so with the first human beings. The first Earth Surface People are generally said to have been made from corn and jewels such as turquoise and white shell, or, from many different elements including soil, lightning, and water (Matthews 1897:136–137; O'Bryan 1956:102–103; Goddard 1933:146–147; Klah 1942:103–107;

---

*The Navajo term *dootł'izh* denotes those segments of the color spectrum referred to by the English terms, blue and green, so that the green hues of plant life may properly be attributed to *niłch'i dootł'izh*, translated here as Blue Wind.

Curtis 1907:96). Whatever the elements used, they were, by various accounts, given life by means and processes similar to those used in giving life to the inner forms of natural phenomena and to other Holy People: Wind gave the corn "the breath of life" (Matthews 1897: 136–137); the Five Chiefs of the Wind sent the Little Breeze which entered the corn and fetishes after which they became human beings (O'Bryan 1956:102–103); *nitch'i biyázhí*, translated by Goddard as smoke but more generally translated as Wind's Child, passed through them enabling them to stand erect (Goddard 1933:147); and, by Curtis' account, people formed when Spirit Winds blew between the skins where the various elements had been laid and Talking God and Calling God had tapped the skins with rainbows and sunbeams (Curtis 1907:96).

In other accounts of the creation of human beings, the material for the creation is said to have been the epidermis of Changing Woman's body along with such jewels as white shell, turquoise, abalone, and jet (e.g., Matthews 1897:147–148; Curtis 1907:96–97; Franciscan Fathers 1910:356; Haile 1930:447–448). Such material was molded into human form and then given life in a ritual during which the breath or speech of Changing Woman was blown upon them, or Wind People or Spirit Wind entered into them (Haile 1930:447–448; Wyman 1970:633; Curtis 1907:96–97; Wyman et al. 1942:14–15).

A singular account by informant CAB assigns to the same Dark Wind and Blue Wind, which "lying on one another" had given life and guidance to the Holy People in the underworlds, an instrumental role in giving life to the Navajo in the present worlds. These Winds, alternatively referred to in this account as Holy Wind and *bik'eh hózhǫ́*, respectively, are said to have gone to the base of the sacred mountain of the west:

> These two people, the one that is Holy Wind and the one that is *bik'eh hózhǫ́*, went there (to the west). They brought corn back and the epidermis of the one who resides over there, Changing Woman. When they took care of the corn it ripened.... They gathered its pollen. It was put inside of the people (who were being created). It was put on them. Then the corn that was white was divided. One of the Mud People (a clan name) was made and also one of the Tall House People. The corn that was yellow was then divided. The Bitter Water People and the Near Water People were then made.... They were prepared to the point where they were ready to get up. "Medicine will be made again," it was said. Then corn pollen was put on us.... The two who went to Changing Woman, Dark Wind and Blue Wind, this way (was said to them):

"You two who went there will be put within them. You (clan people) will talk by means of one lying on the other," it was said "Alright," it was said again. Then the two that went over there entered inside of the people who were made.[16] (CAB)

Some versions indicate not only that those created from Changing Woman's body were the founders of specific Navajo clans but also that a different Wind entered each such clan founder:

Dark Wind was placed within the one called Near Water. Blue Wind was placed within the Tall House one. Again, Yellow Wind (was placed within) the Tall House one (the informant probably did not intend to repeat the name of the Tall House one. The Bitter Water people may have been omitted from this account). White Wind (was placed within) Mud People. So these four were placed separately within them and they live by these. (FDT)

A similar conception was expressed by Wheelwright's informant whose version also tells of the placement of Winds in white people (Wheelwright 1949:57–59). Most accounts, however, do not associate particular Winds with specific clans or groups of people.

In view of the legends of the creation of Earth Surface People, it is understandable that the Navajo can say that they are made of the same elements as are other aspects of this world. "This vegetation with which we will live, this that we exist on top of (the Earth) those mountains, what the Sun is made of, we were made in the same way as these" (informant CAB). But the Navajo conceives himself as being structured most like the Earth which has soil similar to the flesh, stone parts similar to bone, Dawn's dew likened to bodily moisture, and the blessing-giving power of *sǫ'ǫh naagháí* within (Haile 1930:347). For *sǫ'ǫh naagháí*, the primary source of blessings from within the Earth, was put up on Earth's surface for the Navajo to live by, too: "The one called *sǫ'ǫh naagháí*, the one called *bik'eh hózhǫ*, stand within us. They made us, they speak for us, they exist within us."[17] (CM)

GUIDANCE FROM THE FOUR DIRECTIONS

The necessary conditions for Navajo life were established when the natural phenomena of the present world had been endowed with inner forms and with Winds as their means of life, thought, speech, movement, and communication with others for they had then acquired the means of guiding and regulating human life. This conception is broadly set forth in River Junction Curly's version of Blessingway: "'With everything having life, with everything having the power of speech, with everything having the power to breathe, with everything having the power to teach and guide, with that in blessing we will live,' it was said." (Wyman 1970:616).

Earth, Sky, Sun, and Moon are regarded as being important regulators of human life, having strong Winds by which to lead people:

> Three or four really strong persons lead us. This Earth is a very wise woman who owns absolutely every last, breathing thing. The one existing here, within Earth, which she breathes by, is very strong it seems. Over there it is the same with the Sky.[18] (CM)

The Sun is said to regulate peoples' daily activities and thoughts, telling them when to sleep, to eat, to rest:

> He knows what you are thinking and what you do. When he gets to the west he tells you to eat, rest, read and bathe. The Sun suggests or sends thoughts to you telling you to do these things. The wrong people who have the wrong thoughts go by the supreme devil, *bịịh yinłt'áai,* who tells them the wrong things to do (Fishler 1953:21).

It is perhaps through its regulation of the cardinal light phenomena and their inner forms that the Sun influences peoples' daily thoughts and behavior, for the daily journey of the Sun determines the sunwise sequence of these phenomena. Dawn appears ahead of the Sun; following is Sky Blue over which the Sun journeys; Twilight is seen behind the Sun; and, the Sun returns to the east under Darkness (Wyman 1970:372). The inner form of the cardinal light phenomena, in turn, being endowed with the ability to think and to plan, directly regulate human activities. By Frank Mitchell's account it was said that Dawn which is male will be the first to cause people to move and that it will exist exclusively for whatever is good. Sky Blue is female and guides people in going abroad, but being two-sided some bad things happen at that time. Evening Twilight being male is also good since it guides people in coming together again. Darkness is female and there is more of whatever is bad at this time than in the others. It was said that the thinking of these four beings of the cardinal points will be in favor of those people who address them and pray and sing to them in the proper way (Wyman 1970:369–371; cf. Slim Curly's account, pp. 164–165).

Other informants express their views of the influences of the cardinal light phenomena in terms of their effects upon human thought:

> Over here (in the east) Dawn Man, Sky Blue Woman (in the south), over here (in the west) Twilight Man, over here (in the north) Dawn Woman. These make us think. We think according to them.
>
> From where thinking just begins, that is Rolling Darkness. Dawn Boy follows it. Dawn Boy is when it dawns. You rest until that time, then you awaken usually feeling refreshed and well. Then when the Sun is about to rise there is sunlight, the good one shines on us. We think by that.[19] (CAB)

In part, such statements as the foregoing merely reflect the common human experience: we frequently awaken (our thoughts are stirred) before dawn, with dawn we are usually well rested and have a feeling of well-being, daylight is the time of maximum activity and can bring either good or ill fortune, twilight is a good time because we gather together again after our day's activity, and bad things can happen in the darkness and bring bad thoughts. However, there is an additional dimension to the Navajo conception which attempts to account for this variance in human thoughts and happenings from one part of the day to another. A thought, whether for good or ill, never occurs without cause, a Wind is always behind it. The variance in human thoughts throughout the day is accounted for by the activity of different Winds. Thus, the fact that bad things happen during Darkness is due to the Wind associated with it: "Evil happens within Darkness. People who are foolish get their Wind from there."[20] And, if we awaken feeling ill it is because Dark Wind exists with Darkness. It seems that it causes it" (informant CAB).

In the same way, some people do not plan well because they have a bad Wind standing alongside them called Rolling Darkness Wind, while others have a good Wind beside them called Dawn Boy. Here, it seems that informant CM has applied names of aspects of the cardinal light phenomena to the Winds conceived to be existing within them:

> Some people have a bad one (Wind) standing beside them and they do not plan well, even when a really good one stands within them. There are two different Winds, one being good, one being bad. Their names are different, the good Wind is called Dawn Boy, the bad Wind is called Rolling Darkness Wind.[21] (CM)

Thus far has been outlined the Navajo conception of a world on Earth's surface composed of natural phenomena given life and the powers of thought and knowledge and having the capacity of guiding and regulating human life through the action of Wind. The means by which Wind is thought to have effects upon human action remain to be described.

It is Wind conceptualized as Little Wind or Wind's Child that is thought to be sent to Earth Surface People as Messenger of the inner forms of various natural phenomena. Such Messenger Winds are said to be sent by their leaders in the four directions to inform, advise, and protect people and to report back on peoples' conduct. Thus, Winds move Navajo thought at the direction of these leaders:

> These (Winds) move it, the same ones move it (our thinking). The one who is their leader sits (and sends them) from there: from there where the Sun rises, (and) one from over here in the south; one from over there where the Sun sets, (and) one from over there (in the north). So from four directions these (Winds) are here by their direction.[22] (CAB)

Messenger Winds sent by the inner forms of the sacred mountains function very much as agents for those leaders:

> There are leaders inside of the surrounding mountains. Everything valuable will be seen against them (i.e., the mountains are adorned with all desirable things). In this way, these were placed within these mountains. It is just like Washington, D.C. in the white way—agents come from there. In just that same way these Winds are from those foremost leaders placed within the mountains.[23] (CM)

In Slim Curly's version of the Blessingway myth there is the implication that the "chiefs" who send the "messengers" may be found in other places as well:

> And these Holy People are found in many places so, while those that are chiefs as it were stay in their homes, they have many messengers going out from there. These messengers [always on the alert] sit facing you here while you plead [pray]. This news they bring back to the homes of their chiefs where they relate of you, "Clearly he is pleading when he says, I have made your sacrifice [offering]" (Wyman 1970:238).

The next chapter will give further details of the influences of these Messenger Winds on human thought and behavior in the context of a general discussion of the dynamics of behavior from the traditional Navajo point of view.

In review of accounts in the Navajo oral traditions of the creation of the present world on Earth's surface, a number of Navajo beliefs relating to the Wind concept have been brought into focus. It has been seen that Winds, which provided life and guidance to the inhabitants of the underworlds, are conceived to have emerged from below with the other Holy People or to have been placed here by Earth. Particular note should be made of the "Winds lying on one another" which were earlier said to have provided guidance to the Holy People in the underworlds. It is indicated that these now were placed with two other Winds in the cardinal directions from where they enter Earth Surface People during reproductive processes.

As was the case in the underworlds, the Winds of the four directions are closely associated on Earth's surface with the cardinally placed phenomena of light and the principal mountains bordering the Navajo world. From these four directions Wind gives the means of life, movement, thought, and communication to the natural forms of this world including Earth, Sky, Sun, Moon, animals and plants, and to Earth Surface People including the Navajo. Natural phenomena are therefore considered to be alive, no less than the people of this world, and able to communicate with others.

The natural phenomena, having been endowed with inner forms and Wind by which they live and think, are thereby considered to be equipped to provide guidance and instruction to the Navajo. They are thought to do this by means of Winds in the form of Wind's Child or Little Winds which are sent primarily by the Holy Ones in the cardinal directions to influence human thought and conduct. Wind, a unitary being, performs these and other functions under diverse names that are assigned in terms of such criteria as its direction of origin, locus, size, appearance, character, and direction of rotation at any given time and place.

PRINCIPLES
of LIFE &
BEHAVIOR

Discussions in the preceding chapters of the traditional Navajo conceptual structure of the world, of some of the holy powers believed to exist in it, and of the relationships of these powers with one another and the Navajo, prepare for explication of Navajo views of the part played by these Holy Ones in lending direction to the life of the individual. These beliefs concern the roles of the Holy Ones and of Winds in particular in the individual's conception, prenatal development, birth, growth, modes of thought and behavior, and final decline into death. Particular attention is given to behaviors and personal characteristics that are attributed to the direction of Winds sent to the individual by the Holy Ones and those attributed to the influence of other, harmful, powers and Winds. Intrinsic to these aspects of Navajo psychology are beliefs about the nature and source of the moral sense and about the scope of responsibility for one's actions. The final concern of this chapter is the Navajo classification of behaviors that appears to be based on this "Wind theory."

CONCEPTION AND PRENATAL DEVELOPMENT

Wind is believed to be within the individual from the moment of conception, its movement and growth producing movement and growth of the foetus in which it exists. This "Wind within one" may be said to be formed from two, four, twelve, or possibly other numbers of elements. It would seem that Wind from all four directions must be conceived to be within each person. As may be recalled, informant CAB told that Mother Earth in speaking four Words put up one Wind in the east "which directs our life," another in the south which is "our power of movement," one in the west which is "our thinking," and one in the north which is "when we carry out our plans," all four of which would seem to be required for life and behavior. As noted in the previous chapter, these four are but different aspects of a single Wind that suffuses all living things. They are not different:

> They are just one. The one standing within us by means of which we talk is just one. It derives from them. They are just one but are called by different names.[24] (CAB)

Another informant expressed the same concept in this way:

> The elders said that according to the Navajo way there are four ... the one called Dark Wind, the one called Blue Wind, the one called Yellow Wind, the one called White Wind. These four are the ones by which we breathe. Also (i.e., they also said that) we breathe by means of just one although we breathe by means of four.[25] (HB)

The key elements of this Wind for human life appear to be those which were originally put up in the east and in the south, respectively, Word One and Word Two, called also *álílee naagháii* (or *sǫ'ǫh naagháí*) and *bik'eh hózhǫ́:*

> When a baby is going to be formed there (inside its mother), one is already inside it, two being connected together. Over here, the one that is standing within us, the main part, that is *álílee naagháii* and next, on this side, *bik'eh hózhǫ́.*[26] (CAB)

One of this pair of Winds is thought to have come from each of the parents of the child-to-be via his and her body fluids (see p. 23). The female part of the Wind formed at the time of conception is called *álílee naagháii* by informant CAB and *sǫ'ǫh naagháí* by informant CM. The male part, *bik'eh hózhǫ*, is also referred to as Little Wind by informant CAB:

> *Álílee naagháii* moves us. The one called Little Wind is *bik'eh hózhǫ*. That moves us, we live according to it....So in this way, on one another placed, the Little Wind is placed on top of this *álílee naagháii,* so we talk.[27] (CAB)

Four months after conception this Wind within the foetus grows, causing the first movements of the unborn child. Other Wind is added on to that already "standing within" so that it keeps growing along with the foetus:

> Four months after conception the one standing within it moves upwards. When it moves upwards then it (the foetus) moves.... It seems that it (Wind) goes into what is already placed within it (i.e., into the Wind already placed within the foetus). As growth continues it moves. In this way, from then on it keeps growing, growing, growing to the point that it will be born.[28] (CAB)

When the baby is born it is said that the Wind within it "unfolds him." It is at this point that the infant commences breathing on his own and emits his first cry. Surrounding Wind is added on to that within the infant:

> The one that is the very best "wind" adds on to itself those from there, and the one that is *bik'eh hózhǫ* is the same way.[29] (CAB)

The particular Wind that is taken in by the newborn infant is conceived to have a determinative effect on the course of that individual's life, different Winds being sent by the Holy One to different individuals at the time of their birth:

> It (the Holy One) places some good in-standing ones it seems. It places some to so far (i.e., some will exist within people only to a certain point in their lives), some that will make white hair. Different ones, not just one, are placed within. Even though many are born, nevertheless different ones are placed within them it seems.[30] (JD)

Other Winds enter at later points in the development of the individual so that the growing child is believed to be continually subject to the influence of Winds existing around him. This is suggested by the use of the phrase "the Wind standing within one" to refer to Wind that has been breathed in as well as the Wind that one was born with:

> That within us stands from our mouth downwards it seems. We breathe by it. It moves absolutely all of our blood vessels; it moves all parts of our body. We live by it. It moves all parts, even our heart.[31] (HB)

The individual's growth is governed by Wind, and such faculties as speech and the ability to maintain balance and upright posture are also attributed to it:

> We Navajo live by this Wind. When one is in his mother's womb, there he starts to develop at a certain rate. When he finishes developing he is born. From then, according to it (Wind), when he reaches a certain age he will talk. One grows by this Wind, according to its direction.[32] (HB)
>
> It is only by means of Wind that we talk. It exists at the tip of our tongues.[33] (CM)
>
> There are whorls here at the tips of our fingers. Winds stick out here. It is the same way on the toes of our feet, and Winds exist on us here where soft spots are, where there are spirals. At the tops of our heads some children have two spirals, some have only one, you see. I am saying that those (who have two) live by means of two Winds. These (Winds sticking out of the) whorls at the tips of our toes hold us to the Earth. Those at our finger tips hold us to the Sky. Because of these, we do not fall when we move about.[34] (CM)

According to the Navajo conception, then, Winds exist all around and within the individual, entering and departing through respiratory organs and whorls on the body's surface. That which is within and that which surrounds one is all the same and it is holy:

> From there, the one called Holy Wind and Wind *álílee naagháii* stands within us. This same one turns that one that walks about (the Sky?), I say. It turns this (Earth), I say. It turns water, everything. It alone is our Holy One. Really, only it is our prayer.[35] (CAB)

In this way, each individual partakes of the Wind around him. It is both within and all around him:

The one called Wind's Child, this is just like living in water (i.e., it is all around us). This same Wind moves us.... You see, the same Wind's Child exists within our tissues, it moves us, it causes us to think.[36] (GES)

DETERMINANTS OF APPROVED BEHAVIOR

It was seen that in the creation of the world on Earth's surface, the Holy People, existing as inner forms of natural phenomena of the cardinal directions, were given the means of communicating with others by means of Winds. These Winds could be sent as their "messengers," their "means of knowing things" and of providing guidance to Earth Surface People. The Wind within and about the developing individual consists, in part, of such Messenger Winds conceived of as Little Winds or Wind's Child which exist within the Wind that is everywhere there is life. It is these Little Winds sent by the Holy Ones that are thought to provide the means of good Navajo thought and behavior.

There are several forms in which such Messenger Winds are conceived to be received by the individual. In many accounts these Winds are placed at the earfolds from where they may give advice and warning to the individual. Two such "means of knowing" are commonly said to be given to each person, being referred to as Wind or Wind's Child and Darkness or Child of Darkness. It has been told that when First Man found the infant Changing Woman he lifted her up "... recognizing that her mother was Darkness and her father was Dawn, and he noticed that in her right ear was a small White Wind, and in her left a Dark Wind. They had been placed there by her father and mother" (Wheelwright 1949:53). Later in this same text the White Wind is referred to as Little Wind and the Dark Wind is called Child of Darkness, both of whom would warn Changing Woman when her husband was approaching (Wheelwright 1949:57). In the origin legend recorded by Matthews, Wind at the protagonist's ear warned him of dangers by day and Darkness at his left ear warned him by night (Matthews 1897: 100–101). Frank Mitchell said that by means of Darkness and Wind the Holy People are said to be present whenever the Blessingway ceremonial is conducted (Haile 1930:563). Informant GES reaffirmed this belief of singers of Blessingway: "Behind me is Child of Darkness, beside me is Wind's Child. We live by these it seems."

By other accounts, Wind's Children or Little Winds existing in the Winds from all four of the cardinal directions have the capacity of speaking into the ear. Black Mustache related that when First Woman's mother gave birth to two boys and two girls, four very small persons came to them saying, "In days to come things will be known by means of us...." These were identified as "the young one of the Dark Wind," "the young one of the Blue Wind," "the young one of the Yellow Wind," and "the young one of the White Wind." These were placed along the folds of their ears, and it was ordered that in the future it was to be in that way (Haile 1932c:18). Similarly, informant BY indicated that Little Winds are in the Winds from the four directions which are all about one. When Winds are depicted in sandpaintings of the Navajo Windway ceremonial, Little Winds are depicted at their (Wind's) ears talking to them; and, in the same manner, these Little Winds speak into the ears of people:

> To this day, these (Little Winds) exist with all of them, the ones that are Dark Winds, Blue Winds, the ones that are Yellow Winds, the ones that are White Winds. So now when Winds are drawn in sandpaintings these (Little Winds) are made like that, at their earfolds talking to them. Ours sort of copy them, it was given to us in the same way as on the sandpaintings.[37] (BY)

Two informants indicated that Wind's Child or Little Wind no longer directly advises the Navajo through the ear in the way that it advised the Holy People although it may still communicate with the Navajo by other means. In saying that the power of communication which was given by Wind had been taken away from the Navajo, informant JT compared it with the telephone:

> It (Wind) is like the telephone that the white man—everybody, we too!—always picks up to talk to one another, saying "uh huh, uh huh." They say that we, too, used to have Wind. That by which people talked to each other in our way was taken back from us.[38] (JT)

Similarly, informant JD, having related how Little Wind advised the legendary War Twins in their campaign against various "monsters" who were killing off the people, said that after all the monsters had been slain this Wind ceased to give such advice to the people. "At the point when the monsters ceased to exist it stopped. From that time on there has been nothing." Even so, according to this informant, Little Winds are still all around. They tell Coyote what is happening and it is for this reason that if a coyote crosses one's path this should be taken as a warning not to proceed any further. Also, through owls and by other means the Navajo are warned of danger by Little Winds.

It is sometimes said that Winds "stand alongside of us" warning of dangers:

> Here Winds stand alongside of us, one on each side. These tell us, "One who thinks in an evil way is standing looking at you from over there," it seems they say. They keep watch over there.[39] (CM)

These Winds may also be said to stand within one. It is important to understand that such in-standing Winds are also sent by the Holy Ones. Far from being Wind Souls which are "in-dwelling" from birth to death, they are essentially the same as Winds situated at the ear-folds or standing alongside one. The identity between these Winds becomes evident from statements by various informants:

> The same one that stands within us sticks out here (the ears) it seems. We breathe by the same one. That one, Little Wind, stands within us. They exist in all of those that are sounding around here (here, the informant is referring to the high winds which were heard outside of his home on the day of this interview). The same one that stands within us sticks out of our ear-folds (i.e., is placed there), and it is also here at our fingertips (at the whorls which are generally conceived to be tracks left by the entry of Winds into the body).[40] (BY)

Similarly, Sandoval told that when the Navajo was created the Five Chiefs of the Wind sent the Little Breeze, which had been seated at the ears of the Holy People, to enter into those who were being created (O'Bryan 1956:55;102–103). In like manner, informant GES used the terms that are usually used to identify the Wind informant placed at the ear, Wind's Child, to refer to the Wind within one, saying too that it exists everywhere: "Wind's Child exists everywhere. The same Wind's Child exists within us in our tissues. We live by it, we think by it."

It also helps to recall in this connection informant JT's version of events in the underworlds in which Wind both advised the Holy People through their ears and gave them life from within. In the words attributed to Woman Leader, "... within us it is placed and to us it speaks" (see above, p. 00). Wind is here referred to as a single being who performed diverse functions, including those which are distributed among several Winds in other accounts. This unity of Wind as a single entity and deity requires repeated emphasis in view of the Navajo practice of naming its various aspects (see above, pp. 17–18). The basic cocept to be appreciated is that Holy Ones identified with the cardinal directions send Wind to the individual at birth and to provide the means of life and guidance all throughout the individual's life: "Those that are our Holy Ones put them within us. ... All of them were put in this way (within us) and around here among us."[41] (BY)

These Winds sent by the Holy Ones throughout an individual's life are conceived to be the primary source of good thought and behavior. Each person is said to be born with a good Wind within him.[42] (CAB) As the individual grows he may make youthful mistakes, but this Wind within functions to show him where he has not behaved properly, thereby teaching the right way in which to live:

> Thoughtlessness is greater during boyhood. At that time there is a really good one standing within, but nevertheless they (young people) misbehave. It (the Wind within one) teaches one to think about his misbehavior.... It is as though in thinking about this misbehavior it shows it back to oneself. The one that stands within does this: "This is what you did! Don't do that! Here, you look at it!" it seems to tell one about these wrong doings..... So there his thoughts grow within and his Wind grows, too, it seems.[43] (CM)

The ability of the Wind within one to perform this function is, in part at least, contingent upon the individual having received proper instruction from his parents or other socializing agents and strengthening his mind by thinking about and following these teachings:

> What they say about "his mind is strong" is that when one makes himself that way, when something tries to harm him then his mind is really firm. If he doesn't do that then his mind is not stable, his mind is not strong, the one standing within him (his Wind) is not strong. ... If one is taught in that way (the right way), if he thinks about it, if he is wise, he looks at everything in terms of this, it is as though others' actions are projected on a screen. If the one he walks by and breathes by (his Wind) is strong, then everyday it is as though it flicks (like a movie) to him, "That should not be done, you shouldn't do that!"[44] (CL)

The very fact that good instruction is given to an individual is itself due to the influence of Wind on the socializing agents:

> The same one that walks around for you (i.e., the Wind that is sent here to help you) is sent also to them (one's parents). Then they teach the baby by means of it. They give instruction to the one that is born by means of the good one, they were taught by means of the good Wind.[45] (CAB)

Winds sent by the Holy Ones, then, are conceived to influence both an individual and his instructors to conduct themselves in the right way. They work hard to keep the Wind within one strong, even replacing it when it has become tired. They report what one says to the east and receive messages from there which are passed on as warnings and advice:

> When our thinking, the one that stands within us, becomes tired, this Little Wind sends others from there so that our thinking is strong, the one standing within us is strong. It takes it out (i.e., the one that became tired). It does not give up for us. It reports from here to the east like a radio; what I am saying now is heard over there. In that way it is received from it (Little Wind) over there; and then from there, "This way!" it tells it (i.e., the Holy One in the east tells this to Little Wind to relay back to us). In this way we think.[46] (CAB)

The Navajo traditionalist conceives, then, that the Wind with which he is born and the Winds that are sent from the four directions to take care of him work together as constituent parts of Holy Wind to protect him from harmful outside influences. By this means he is shown the right way to behave and is warned of dangers. What is believed to be characteristic of a person whose life is governed by these influences is that he is responsive to good instruction and observes and follows the good ways of others. By means of good instruction and a strong Wind it is said that "he lacks faults": "When he thinks by means of the one by which he becomes wise, when he lives in a helpful way, he is lacking in faults."[47] (CL)

It is worthwhile to examine the meaning of the phrase "one who lacks faults" in order to be able to specify the personal qualities that are attributed to the influences of helpful Wind sent by the Holy Ones. One's faults or lack of them are conceived to be manifested in all facets of behavior, in thought, speech, and action.* It is said that one who lacks faults "thinks in a good way," "thinks carefully," "thinks in a nice way about one" and so on. Speech follows thought in Navajo ideology, and it is said that one who lacks faults "talks in a nice way" and "his language is good." Finally, it is said of one who lacks faults that "he walks in a good way" or "he lives in a good way." Consider, further, the attributes of one who lacks faults:

> This person who lacks faults thinks in a good way, he thinks well of one, one thinks well of him. He usually smiles, comes up to one slowly and, showing his relationship, shakes one's hand. (HB)
> "One lacks faults" means ... he does not argue with a person. He does not steal. He is not mean.... Nothing bad is said about him. He is obliging towards everything. (CM)

Being "obliging" refers to a willingness to help others:

> It is not spoken in vain towards him.... Ask him something and he will help out, this person who is very obliging. (HK)

One who lacks faults is also characterized as being thoughtful. This refers to the ability to think expansively and to show good judgement: "They speak well. They think about everything. All of their plans are broad. All of their counsel is farsighted." A quality of even-temperedness is also characteristic of a person who is under the protection of Wind sent by the Holy Ones:

> Sometimes another person, when quarreling with a person who lacks what is called faults, sasses him in vain: "I will argue strongly with him, (and) he will speak in a bad way," (thinks the) one in whom bad words exist (but he) wishes in vain. That person who lacks faults says nothing in this way. Even if one says something to that one, he will not get angry. (CM)

---

*Haile's data first suggested that "lacking in faults" and "having faults" may be generic Navajo categories which are inclusive of more specific behavioral traits (Haile 1943). While this taxonomy was confirmed by informant GES, other informants would likely give alternative taxonomies of behavioral categories. The data are sufficient, however, to support a bipartite division between those traits associated with "lacking faults" and those associated with "having faults," whatever the head taxa might turn out to be.

DETERMINANTS OF DISAPPROVED BEHAVIOR

Just as Messenger Winds from the Holy Ones are thought to be the primary source of good conduct, so wrong conduct is attributed to the influence of harmful or evil Winds on an individual. The strength of the inner Wind, the stage of a person's development when evil Winds exert their influence, the nature of these evil Winds, and the ways in which they influence other persons in the individual's environment are all factors that are considered to be of significance in determining the course of the individual's behavior. The behavioral characteristics of those under the influence of evil Winds are clearly defined by the Navajo and are contrasted with the characteristics of those under the influence of good Winds.

Reference was made in the previous chapter to the formation of various Winds on Earth's surface when the present world was being created, some of which were said to cause bad things and problems to happen (see above, pp. 16–17). Some evil Winds are Ghosts that have departed from the bodies of the dead:

> This matter of not speaking good words, well when we die, the one that stands within us (the Wind within) leaves. It does not die. It walks out of one who did not talk in the right way, becoming a Ghost. So after the Wind that left a person rises among those right here, then one's words are not good.[48] (CAB)

It can be told whether a Wind which departed from a body is good or bad by the direction in which it is rotating:

> The evil one is called Rolling Darkness. The good Wind is called just Darkness. A person dies when evil thoughts or something bad happens. After that it runs out and mixes with them. When looking at this Wind, the good one turns sunwise (i.e., in the same direction as the sun is conceived to travel). The evil one that ran out turns sunward (i.e., in the direction opposite to the sun's movement).[49] (CM)

Ghosts, then, may exist in the form of harmful whirlwinds. Various kinds of whirlwinds may affect one's conduct adversely:

> There are so many different kinds of these Winds that run around here. One is called Striped Wind. Again, one is called Coiled Wind. One is Revolving Wind. If these run to here (to

whomever is affected), they usually say of him that he does not live in the right way. That Wind does it. It talks in a bad way for him. It is as though it is saying to him from there, "Say this!"[50] (CAB)

These whirlwinds have their effect by changing the character of the Wind within one: "If the sunward Wind runs upon us, running within us, then we think just any way. . . . . It makes the Wind that we had lived by act erratically."[51] (FDT) If this happens in early childhood so that the growing child is under the continuous influence of bad Winds there may be no way to restore the original condition:

Only good ones are put within us but when we start crawling around the Winds that run around are put on us. . . . These evil ones are put on what was growing nicely before, so one grows in that way with them. There is usually no cure.[52] (CAB)

It is commonly held by informants that bad Winds do not respect any subgroup of the Navajo population. Any family may have a member who comes to have a bad Wind within him. No matter how adequate and favorable home conditions and parental guidance are, there are differences among children in terms of their responses to these conditions and to parental injunctions. Those who do not listen have bad Winds within them:

Some live recklessly, some carefully follow teachings. . . . Of so many boys, say five, some drink, some think about life. . . . The ones standing within them are probably different. It seems that these do this to them.[53] (HK)

So, the Wind within one, when harmful Winds impinging upon the individual are incorporated into it, causes a change in the individual's behavior from good to bad:

Sometimes we generally talk in a very nice way. Then we turn to another way of speaking, the words being different. The same Wind that stands within us causes this.[54] (CAB)

A critical factor disposing one's Wind to produce bad thoughts and bad talking is its lack of strength. A weak Wind within one is more susceptible to being influenced by evil Winds from without:

> Over there it seems an evil one is waiting. Here, the one that
> he really lived by seems to stop (working). Then the evil Wind runs
> in here (between the eyes).* At this point bad things happen.[55]
> (CM)

But the effects of such harmful Winds may even overrule the
potentiality for good of a strong Wind within an individual:

> Some it seems have a bad one which stands on them. They
> do not plan well even when a really good one possessing every-
> thing stands within them.[56] (CM)

Sometimes if one's thoughts and behavior are changed for the
worse another human agent may be the cause, although a Wind
determines the latter's action. Witchcraft appears to be involved:
"From a Wind over there that makes one act, a man who had bad
thoughts wishes, 'I will cause something [bad to happen]!'"[57] (CM)

The bad thoughts of another person can be placed within one so
that the latter's former good thinking is ruined:

> One is living in a good way, thinking in a good way, thinking
> pleasant thoughts. Then those who think badly, those whose talk
> is bad, replace everything within us, so they re-run in us. It ruins
> one's life, one's thinking, everything. So it is said that one just
> walks in confusion. That is not good.[58] (GES)

A young informant explained that by means of certain kinds of
witchcraft practices a person can take away another's Wind and re-
place it with a bad one, or get control of it and cause it to make its
possessor behave in ways harmful to himself or others. Alternatively,
the Winds of dangerous animals can be controlled and used to cause
those animals to engage in destructive acts against other people. A
person wishing to harm another in such ways must be cautious,
however, for if the latter has a strong Wind within him then he will
overpower the one who intends harm:

> These Winds over there, Earth's Wind, Sky's Wind, and Sun
> and Moon (their Winds), these are highly valued.... These four
> are dangerous.... If a person lives by means of them and one
> thinks here in a bad way of him, it will not happen. The bad
> thinking will not go his way. One will merely fall under him.[59] (CM)

---

*The entrance of the evil Wind between the eyes, as indicated by the informant's
gestures, is possibly related to the Navajo conception of the nose as being a seat of
thought.

Just as it is characteristic of a person having a good Wind within him that he learns the right way to live in accordance with the example and teachings of others, so it is characteristic of a person under the influence of bad Winds that he does not listen to what he is told and does not generally benefit from instruction:

> Because of it (a bad Wind within him) he does not do what he is told, they say to themselves. He usually talks in any old way. (CM)

In the same way that a person having a good Wind within him is said to be lacking in faults (see p. 40), it is said of one who lives by a bad Wind that he has faults:

> When a person thinks in the right way, is not reckless, does not talk just any old way, it is said that he lacks faults. This one who is reckless and who talks just in any way has faults. The one that stands within him leads him to think in that way, it seems.[60] (FTD)

Again, such faults are manifested in thought, speech, and behavior. One who has faults thinks in a bad way, he does not think very far ahead, his thoughts are not very strong, and so forth. In his speech such a person talks in just any way, his language is bad, he talks carelessly, etc. In his actions he does not walk in a good way. The behavioral effects attributed to harmful Winds can be specified by further analysis of the meaning of one's faults:

> In the Navajo way, if he is lazy, if he does not do what he is told, it seems from that he is mean.... He speaks carelessly. This person has faults.
> In the Navajo way, it is usually said of one who drinks, one who is quick-tempered and fights with people, that he has faults.

Thus, as was seen earlier, while one who is under the protection and influence of Messenger Winds sent by the Holy Ones lacks faults, benefits from instruction, has a thoughtful approach towards life, is well-disposed and helpful towards others, and is even-tempered and difficult to anger; one who is under the influence of harmful Winds has faults, is contrary and argumentative, and is quick-tempered to the point of being mean and intemperate in his actions.

This theory of behavior, which attributes one class of personal characteristics to the effects of one class of Winds and another class of personal characteristics to the effects of a second class of Winds, also conceptualizes Winds as having the same characteristics of which they are the cause in humans (Haile has previously pointed this out in his article on Navajo "soul concepts": 1943). Thus, it is said of a Wind, as well as of a person, that it either lacks faults or has faults:

> The good Wind existing among us, the one which turns sunwise lacks faults. The one which turns sunward has faults.
>
> A man who will be good, who will be standing in a good way, has a good Wind forming within him. He lacks faults, he is not reckless, he is helpful toward others.... Again, over here one is not helpful, he is stubborn, he criticizes others, he speaks words that are not good. Back there a Wind that is the same way formed within him.[61] (CM)

COUNTERACTING THE EFFECTS OF EVIL WINDS

While the Navajo Wind theory of behavior provides explanations for both good conduct and wrong conduct in terms of the effects of two different classes of Winds on the individual's behavior, it also specifies ways in which the individual may avoid the undesirable influence of evil Winds and exert some control over his own destiny. These ways include heeding the foreknowledge of evil influences provided by the Little Winds sent from the four directions, and exercising the option to petition these Little Winds to strengthen the Wind within one. If such forewarnings are not heeded or the help of Little Winds is not solicited, evil influences may then gain the ascendancy with disastrous consequences for the individual.

Little Winds from the four directions are thought to help the individual by strengthening the Wind within him, pushing away harmful ones impinging upon him from without, and amply warning him of the future dangers inherent in a given course of action:

> From there it places the good Wind within us by means of which we will speak, and from that point we think for ourselves. And, from there, Little Wind goes around so that we speak by it. It also pushes bad things that will affect us away from us. When it is not watching, it seems, it (the bad one) goes in here so that we become sick. In the same way, by the same one we think ahead for ourselves and speak for ourselves. It puts behind us whatever causes hardship—we think about it and plan for ourselves. For that reason, the one called Little Wind exists here.[62] (CAB)

This Wind not only guides the individual's thinking but also continually monitors his behavior to see if he is living accordingly:

> It is that way with these two placed in (each of) the mountains. Here Winds are placed for us (and) from there they presently move among us. If you do not respect something, if you laugh about a person, if you call a person names, the ones (Winds) that come from the two placed in the mountains send news to there. Over there next is (reported) this: "This person leads his life in *this* way, he said *this*!" In this way these Winds take news back.[63] (CM)

If the person is seen to repeatedly ignore Wind's advice and to "stumble" as a result, Wind may withdraw its support and guidance:

> When (a person) lives in the right way that is good. When he is not living this way, it (Wind) does not like it. I am saying to you that Wind seems to talk to one from there, it makes one think. In the same way that we are telling each other things it seems to talk to one from there, this Wind. It is our thinking, our planning, we live according to it. From there this Wind is our thinking: "I will walk that way!" one wanted (and) so walked. But, walking over here (the other way) he stumbles, and that is not good.[64] (HB)
>
> If one starts walking in the wrong way, it seems that this one called Wind, by which we live, at first wants to save him. "Be careful—do this, do this!" it seems to say when he starts walking that way. If he reaches a certain point in his bad ways, it works very hard for him, thinking in vain, "It should have been this way from a long time back." Then if he again starts walking in that same way, the one called Wind does not lead him through here (i.e., in the right way).[65] (HB)

Whenever it reaches the stage that Winds stop providing guidance, it may be disastrous for the individual:

> These Winds tell things to each other just as we are talking to one another now. So from that point they are talking about him. "Leave him alone, don't bother him, let him do what he wants!" When that happens, that is very bad.[66] (HB)

It seems that what is conceived to happen at the point when Winds withdraw their guidance and support is that the individual becomes weak, and when Wind has finally been taken away he then dies:

> When the one that is Wind from over there thinks of one, if it looks at him and he is not walking this way (the right way), it makes his power of movement, his legs, his appendages weak. In this way the road he was walking on appears dim.... If he cannot seem to straighten himself up, it slows it (his Wind) down, it takes it from us. That is the end.[67] (HB)

A similar conception was expressed by another informant:

> If we are going to make an important mistake, something not good, Winds go about here for information. If we say something bad, we make a mistake in our Navajo way. "It is not good with him," it is said about us. From there, the one that is our Holy One takes out the Wind that was within us. He stops our heart.[68] (CAB)

The individual, then, is conceived to be amply guided and forewarned by Winds sent from the Holy Ones, with the implication that he is given the latitude to live his life accordingly. The individual can also actively petition Wind for its help in counteracting the effects of harmful influences:

> It is listening. We who are Navajo live here by means of it. From here we talk to it. If we plead with it, it hears us. From then on it is good. If something harms one, by that means (i.e., by pleading with Wind) it becomes good. The person gets well.[69] (FDT)

Slim Curly, in his version of the Blessingway legend, indicated that a person may pray and make offerings to the Wind standing within him to induce it to remain with him:

> Pollen Boy you will deposit at the top of your heads with accompanying prayer, and you will give some to your instanding ones accompanied by prayer. On the strength of that they will be satisfied to continue standing within you (Haile 1932a:175).

Similarly, diverse references are made in the Navajo Windway and Chiricahua Windway chantway myths to means by which Winds can be petitioned for their assistance. For example, in Black Mustache's version of the Navajo Windway legend, the prayersticks of Little Winds as well as of the Winds of the four directions are described, and it is indicated that they may be petitioned to restore one's power of movement, thinking, and speech (Haile 1932c:22–23; 120–121). When such prayers are made the petitioner's Wind may again be strengthened and well-being and right thinking may be restored.

If despite the advice and warnings given by Winds sent by the Holy Ones and the availability of their help through prayers and offerings, a person disregards their succorance and persists in a wrong way of life, his Wind may be taken from him, an indication that it is no longer leading him along the good way. It appears to be for this reason that the departed Winds of those who do not live to an old age are to be feared. Their faults, their harmful characteristics, are taken for granted.

Wind is believed to be within the individual from the moment of his conception when two Winds, one from each parent, form a single one within the embryo. The two parts of this Wind are called *są'ąh naagháí* (or *álílee naagháii*) and *bik'eh hózhǫ́* (which is also called Little Wind). This grows with the foetus giving movement to it, and at birth it is added onto by another Wind which enters the infant as he begins to live and breathe. As the child develops under the guidance of the Wind within him, that Wind may be strengthened, weakened, or even replaced by other Winds which impinge upon it from without.

Little Winds sent from the Holy Ones in the four directions work to strengthen the Wind within one towards the end that it will continue to be capable of helping the individual to lead a good life. A person with such a strong Wind characteristically has the capacity to benefit from proper instruction, and it is said that he lacks faults. One having a weak Wind is more vulnerable to the influence of harmful surrounding Winds including those harmful Winds which have departed from the bodies of the deceased and which rotate sunward. These harmful Winds may enter into a person causing him to engage in bad thinking. A person under their influence characteristically does not respond to good instruction, and it is said that such a person has faults.

The Winds sent from the four directions amply provide one with forewarning of harmful influences from surrounding Winds and work hard to protect one from them. Furthermore, they may be petitioned for their assistance. If, in spite of this, an individual does not heed their warnings and advice, the Holy Ones may remove his Wind from him and then he will die.

RETHINKING
NAVAJO
PHILOSOPHY

It has been seen that traditional Navajo culture contains a system of beliefs for explaining and accounting for many of the complexities in the lives and behaviors of Earth Surface People, the human occupants of this world on Earth's surface. That Air or Wind should be a basic concept in the Navajo theory of life and behavior is not unexpected in view of the association of life with breath found in cultures in many parts of the world. However, the manner in which this basic association between life and breath has been developed by the Navajo into a comprehensive theory of life, motion, thought, speech, and behavior has implications for the proper understanding of many issues in Navajo ethnology and, as a case study of traditional theoretical systems, for the ethnology of belief systems in general.

DIFFERENTIATION OF WIND

Since the Navajo conceive of Wind as a unitary being or phenomenon, there being only one Wind which is the source of all life, movement, and behavior, it is of ethnological interest to explore how this basic construct has been elaborated so as to enable it to account for the variance in the observable events requiring explanation. The essential unity of Wind as a single, deified phenomenon has been obscured by its formal differentiation into different aspects that are assigned various causal functions. In Navajo terms, the name by which Wind is called is a function of such criteria as its locus, the color symbolism of the direction of its origin, its size, its direction of rotation, and its possible effects on one at any particular time and place (see pp. 17–18).

The data suggest that Wind has been subcategorized by the Navajo into its constituent parts largely on the basis of what might be called its perceptible properties and only to a much lesser extent on the basis of abstract features having no perceptible manifestations. For the Navajo, who closely identify the four principal Winds with phenomena of light associated with the cardinal directions, the visual properties of these Winds are experientially given. If one will grant the Navajo premises, it can be admitted that the perceptible properties of White Wind, Blue Wind, Yellow Wind, and Dark Wind are manifested in the white of Dawn, the blue of the Sky, the yellow of Twilight, and the dark of Night, respectively. In a similar way, a key distinction in the Navajo theory is between whirlwinds that turn clockwise, in accordance with the conceived motion of the Sun in the east, south, west, north direction, and Winds that turn counterclockwise or contrary to the Sun's movement (see p. 42). Whirlwinds are clearly observable in the Navajo country during the dry, windy seasons of spring and summer, due to the quantities of sand and dirt caught up in their movements. Furthermore, distinctions among Winds on the basis of their size reflect observable phenomena. Wind's Child or Little Wind are key concepts in the Navajo theory of life and behavior, presumably because they are small enough to enter into bodily orifices and inhabit the body (see p. 30). Navajo informants will point to tiny, soot-filled whirlwinds at the base of fireplaces as evidence for the existence of Wind's Child or Little Wind. At the other extreme are strong Winds having very real destructive power, attested to by great sky-obscuring dust storms. Examples of the perceptible properties of Wind could be multiplied. Bad odors emanating from dead animals, or even attributed by the Navajo to the breath of some live animals, are evidence of the presence of potentially harmful Winds. The characteristics of a gentle breeze are manifest to all. Other discriminations between Winds are made on the basis of features which are not so readily apparent. Is there a basis in perception for Striped Wind or for Spotted Wind or do these concepts perhaps result from tinkering with the basic model? Furthermore, while Wind's Child may be at times perceptible in the soot at the base of fireplaces, it is usually not so. A Wind whispering into one's ear is a conception having no known observable referents.

For the Navajo, then, the basic theoretical entity for accounting for life, motion, thought, speech, and behavior has been differentiated so as to account for variance in these events; and, the theoretical grid which has been constructed in terms of attributes of Wind is based in large part upon its perceptible properties in the Navajo environment and only to a lesser extent upon more abstract dimensions, all endowed with some significance in making sense of the world.

RELATIONSHIP OF WIND TO THE INDIVIDUAL

Since Wind is conceived of by the Navajo as a single entity, its postulated relationship to the individual must be seen in the perspective of this understanding.

Navajo Psychology

It is apparent that the Western conception of the soul of an individual, a spiritual agency residing within and imparting life to the individual, fails to translate the Navajo conception of an essentially unitary Wind which envelops the individual throughout life. In interpreting the Navajo view, the individual may more accurately be thought of as participating in this Wind existing everywhere, thereby deriving from it the powers of life, movement, thought, speech, and behavior of which it is the source. That many peoples conceive of such a participation in powers surpassing the individual was recognized by the French philosopher, Lucien Lévy-Bruhl (1971[1927]:115–121, 192–197).

This construction of Wind as an omnipresent entity in which living beings participate best accounts for the available data and synthesizes the interpretations of other ethnologists: Haile's view that Wind within the individual is conceived to be the source of life, movement, speech and behavior; Reichard's recognition that the Wind deity furnishes the breath of life to the individual and that the breath power of other deities can be inhaled or expelled (see p. 2); Witherspoon's assertion that Wind is conceived to be omniscient and omnipresent (Witherspoon 1977: 61) and that it plays a central role in the Navajo universe (see pp. 1–2); and it is not inconsistent with the concept of prehuman flux which Luckert identifies as being dominant in Navajo thought (see pp. 2–3). However, it departs from Haile's view that this Wind is thought to be contained by the body throughout life (see p. 2), and implies a body-spirit dualistic theory of man. With regard to the concept of prehuman flux, if a transformation is conceived to be wrought upon a person by one of the Holy People for an offense incurred, resulting in sickness, it would seem that more than appearances are involved in the transformation; the essences of the Holy Person and the individual must also be somehow involved. When, for example, Coyote "blows his skin" onto a person in order to bring about a transformation, is not the same mechanism involved as when Coyote dispatches his Ghost into one, even though Luckert identifies the latter as a case of dualistic infection rather than the holistic transformation implied by the former? The breath and Ghost of Coyote are both aspects of the Wind within him, and each is capable of transforming the Wind and thus the life and character of the individual who is affected. The holism which Luckert detects in Navajo thought is not, I think, essential to his primary argument which is that the people-like essences of all living beings can assume new appearances. But a transformation of appearance seems to imply transformation of other characteristics as well, if not of the underlying person-like essence then at least of the Wind affecting the life and behavior of that essence.

The individual is conceived to directly participate in what has been identified as the primary source of all beneficent power *(są'ąh naaghái bik'eh hózhǫ)*, as well as in other powers both beneficent and evil (see pp. 15–17). Through participation in the powers of *są' ąh naaghái bik'eh hózhǫ*, the individual is conceived to have direct access to its beneficent powers of life, breath, thought, and speech. When Haile inquired of an informant as to the meaning of the phrase *są'ąh naaghái bik'eh hózhǫ* and was told that it is "the very life and breath" of an individual, he interpreted his informant's response to mean that the meanings of the words are too sacred to be revealed (Haile 1930: Introduction). The present data suggest that perhaps the informant was simply answering his question. Further, since the words *są'ąh naaghái bik'eh hózhǫ* have been identified by Haile and others with the thought and speech of the Holy People, the interpretation offered here is that the individual is able, by participation in these powers, to have direct access to the thought and speech of the Holy Ones. This appears to obviate the necessity of Witherspoon's interpretation that the Navajo seek identification of their thought and speech with *sǫ'ǫh naagháí bik'eh hózhǫ́* in ritual through purely symbolic process (Witherspoon 1977:35–36). That *sǫ' ǫh naagháí bik'eh hózhǫ́* are directly incorporated into the spiritual make-up of Earth Surface People as they are of the Holy People themselves, being productive of sustaining life, breath, thought, and speech for all living things, becomes clear only from the present data, although it relates closely to Reichard's view that the "breath power" of benevolent deities may be directly incorporated through the rite of inhalation (see p. 2). Witherspoon also cites an instance in which *hózhǫ́* may be ritually breathed in by the individual (Witherspoon 1977: 61). A very literal identification with such power is thereby achieved.

The individual is also conceived to participate in other powers as well, some being sent to him from the sacred mountains and others existing about him, all of which exist before and after the individual and yet are potential and real components of his being while he is alive. If Wind is, in Reichard's phrase, an "undependable" deity (Reichard 1970 [1950]:53–72), it is because ugly or evil powers are manifested in it, and these powers may also be incorporated into man to have their effects upon his powers of motion, thought, speech, behavior and general strength and well-being. As with beneficent powers, they may enter during breathing and through bodily orifices or they can influence thought through the ear. This evil aspect of Wind includes Winds which have departed from the bodies of individuals who died prior to attainment of old age. Other Winds may be controlled by means of witchcraft techniques to exert harmful effects. Presumably, the particular Winds associated with hostile deities can convey the powers of these deities to impinge upon the individual. These together with the Winds of dangerous animals and Winds abnormally rotating sunward may, in the manner of the "breath poison" referred to by Reichard, be injurious if they impinge upon one (see p. 2).

Seen in the above context, Navajo psychology posits that personal characteristics are manifestations of similar characteristics existing in the powers of the universe. The complex of behavioral traits subsumed by the term "being faultless" are a function of existing under the influence of aspects of Wind that are also faultless. This Wind is sent to the individual by deities such as Talking Gods and Calling Gods who are inner forms of the sacred mountains and who are themselves absolutely faultless (see p. 19). In the same manner, those undesirable behavioral traits referred to by the term "having faults" are the effects of an aspect of Wind that also has faults (see p. 46). It may be concluded, therefore, that in the same way that health for the Navajo has been said to involve a proper relationship to one's environment and not just the correct functioning of one's physiology (Witherspoon 1974:54), it may also be said that good conduct and character involves such a relationship and is not merely the expression of a good, autonomous self. The dynamic processes underlying good health and good conduct, in the Navajo view, may very well be the same.

Navajo Morality

For the Navajo the moral sense, too, has its source in benevolent supernatural powers, right conduct being an integral part of an ideal relationship with these powers. This interpretation is admittedly at odds with the conclusions of earlier investigators that Navajo morality is independent of the religious system (see p. 4). Yet, it is clear from the present data that Messenger Winds are conceived to be sent to the Navajo by the Holy Ones and that these are thought to convey prescriptions of right conduct. These Messenger Winds, being added on to the Wind already within an individual, thereby help the Wind governing thought and behavior to function, in part, as a conscience, which has been defined in *Webster's International Dictionary of the English Language* (1952) as being "... a faculty, power, or principle, conceived to decide as to the moral quality of one's thoughts, enjoining what is good ...":

> It (the Wind within one) teaches one to think about his misbehavior.... It is as though in thinking about this misbehavior it shows it back to onself. The one that stands within does this: "This is what you did! Don't do that! Here, you look at it!" it seems to tell one about these wrong doings (see p. 39). (CM)

The Holy Ones are believed not only to prescribe right conduct to the Navajo by the medium of Winds but also to enforce their prescriptions. Although Wind may repeatedly warn an individual about his wrong ways, events may finally reach a point where the Winds in essence give up and say among themselves, "'Leave him alone, don't bother him, let him do what he wants!' When that happens, that is very bad" (see p. 47). This is a most serious development in the Navajo view for when such Winds withdraw their guidance and support from the individual, the Wind within him is inevitably weakened and he, himself, thereby weakens. When Wind is finally taken away death results (see p. 47).

The above interpretation appears to be consistent with a Navajo belief in personal responsibility and accountability for one's conduct, contrary to Haile's interpretation cited earlier (see p. 2) The role of Wind is here interpreted to be that of guiding the individual's thought and behavior and repeatedly warning him when necessary of the consequences of his acts. The individual may also be influenced by evil Winds and for that reason not heed the advice, but let it not be said that he lacked forewarning!

Thus, while holiness may not in every instance connote moral sanctity or goodness, nevertheless Navajo knowledge of that which is moral is believed to derive at least in part from the deities. It seems justifiable to conclude that for the Navajo an ideal relationship with the Holy Ones consists in part of living in accordance with their moral principles.

Navajo Eschatology

The death of an individual before the attainment of old age is thought to be brought about by the active intervention of deities. As seen above, they deprive an individual of the Wind within him, his breath of life, in instances in which he persists in living in the wrong way despite warnings and guidance sent by means of Messenger Winds. In such cases, that Wind taken away from the person, presumably the cause of his wrong doings, is subsequently to be feared as a Ghost which exists as a Wind turning sunward among other Winds on Earth's surface (see p. 42).

Such an interpretation agrees with that of Reichard in attributing the cause of death at an early age to the evil the body has been unable to throw off. However, it differs in that the direct cause of death in the present view is an action by one of the deities in finally removing that evil (see p. 48). It also differs from Reichard's as well as Haile's interpretation in identifying the departed evil with the departed Wind, although such an interpretation agrees with that of Wyman and others who describe the identification of the Ghost with the departed Wind Soul as being a major idea pattern in Navajo eschatology (Reichard 1943;354–360; 1970 [1950]:48–49, 120; Haile 1943:87–92; 1951:136; Wyman et al. 1942:11–49).

Living to an old age is a sure indication that the deities had been given no cause by the individual's misconduct to remove his Wind. It may be for this reason that the breath of life is not to be feared by others when, after it declines in strength concurrently with one's attainment of old age, it finally leaves the body.

Navajo World View

Discussions of Navajo world view generally center around the Navajo concern for the maintenance of health and well-being, as expressed in ritual as well as in myth. It is generally accepted that these desired conditions are conceived by the Navajo to derive from the maintenance of harmonious relationships with beneficent supernatural powers. The Navajo phrase *sǫ' ǫh naagháí bik'eh hózhǫ́*, while its meaning has been subjected to diverse interpretation, is thought to symbolize the ideal or goal of beauty, harmony, order and well-being (for discussions of this concept see Haile 1930: Introduction; Reichard 1970 [1950]:45–57, 75–76; Witherspoon 1977:17–40).

While the Navajo may seek to establish the desired conditions of well-being, order, and harmony, there exist, as has been seen, countervailing forces which have the effect of introducing disorder, conflict, and disharmony into the Navajo universe. Yet, it has been noted that the individual can petition the Holy Ones for assistance in counteracting the effects of such harmful influences (see p. 48). Witherspoon, citing the value the Navajo placed on control of their world, emphasizes the role that language plays in achieving such control over supernatural powers:

> It is through language that man acquires the capacity to control the Holy People, the inner forms of powerful natural forces..... Without language man is greatly reduced in stature, and his control of the world about him is greatly impaired. He becomes the acted upon rather than the actor, the created rather than the creator, the object rather than the subject (Witherspoon 1977:80).

In Witherspoon's analysis, Air or Wind plays a central role in the process by which man, through language, acquires control over natural forces; speech is conceived by the Navajo as an externalization of thought, an imposition of form on the external world in which Air is transformed (Witherspoon 1977:31). Thus, surrounding Air, transformed by the Air streaming from the breast of the speaker, becomes the means by which the Holy People are controlled:

> To control the gods, he must raise himself above them.... And because his will is thrust into and imposed upon the omnipotent, omniscient, and omnipresent air in which the god himself lives,

thinks, speaks, and acts, both the singer's and the speaker's will
is done (Witherspoon 1977:61).

In order, then, to reestablish the ideal conditions of beauty, order, harmony, and well-being symbolized by the word *hózhǫ́*, the
individual through ritual creates *hózhǫ́* in his own being and then, in
the speech act, imposes the order, beauty, and harmony expressed by
hózhǫ́ into his universe.

> After a person has projected *hózhǫ́* into the air through ritual
> form, he then at the conclusion of the ritual, breathes that *hózhǫ́*
> back into himself and makes himself a part of the order, harmony,
> and beauty he has projected into the world through the ritual
> mediums of speech and song (Witherspoon 1977:61).

Witherspoon's analysis of the ritual speech act as a means of
realizing the ideal of beauty, harmony, and order is a necessary com-
plement to the analysis in the present study of the role of supernatural powers, by means of Wind, in influencing human thought
and behavior. The focus herein has been on the ways in which the
Holy Ones are thought to exercise surveillance over Navajo behavior,
receiving reports about it by means of Little Winds and issuing injunctions telling how one should think and act. Witherspoon's work
helps to highlight that the present study considers only in passing the
effects of ritual events on the relationship between supernatural
powers and the thought and behavior of the individual.

By the same token, the present data suggest that Witherspoon's
analysis of relationships between the Navajo and the Holy People—
and the central role of the speech act and of Wind in these
relationships—applies best in understanding the special conditions
created by the ritual event. His vision of Navajo control over the gods
(Witherspoon 1977:61), while applicable to the ideal ritual occasion,
does not seem to be descriptive of the man–god relationship in the
everyday world as conceived by the Navajo. There, guidance and
control of the Navajo by supernatural powers, rather than the re-
verse, seems to be the norm.

MYTH AND REALITY

The many ways in which Navajo myth and the theoretical systems based upon it diverge from views of reality as constructed by
modern science are apparent from the vantage point of Western culture. The extent to which causal relations postulated by Navajo
theory express similar relations as postulated by modern science is

less apparent. Comparisons of the two systems of thought should not be expected to reveal identities since the basic theoretical entities differ. However, following Lévi-Strauss' cue that traditional systems of classification as embodied in mythic thought are suitable codes for conveying messages, likened to languages, it is possible to look for ways in which the two languages in question, the Navajo Wind theory and scientific theory explaining the same kinds of events, are conveying similar messages about causal relations (Lévi-Strauss 1966:75–76). It is in this sense that Horton could see expressions of the same reality in psychoanalytic concepts of warring factions within the mind and West African ideas about contesting souls within a body (Horton 1967a:57–58).

It is in this same sense that the Navajo theory appears to hold to some of the basic aspects of the same reality as is expressed in the modern scientific language of, for example, Mischel's social behavior theory which is "... a synthesis of theoretical principles from the experimental study of social behavior and cognition" (Mischel 1968:149). In both theories, the recognition of the saliency of situational or environmental influences on thought and behavior, whether these influences be conceptualized as Winds or as stimuli and reinforcement contingencies, stands in marked contrast to "folk" as well as scientific theories which stress the purely intrapsychic determinants of behavior (Mischel 1968:4–9). If the Wind within one, as an immediate source of thought and behavior, be taken to refer in part to the same reality as an individual's repertoire of acquired or learned behaviors in social behavior theory, then both theories concur that this reality may be weakened or strengthened by means of external influences and experiences. In the same way both theories, generally speaking, regard deviance as being a function of the situational conditions which produce it, whether these be thought of as stimulus conditions or as harmful Winds, rather than of intrapsychic pathology (Mischel 1968:150–201). Accordingly, both theories stress modification of the individual's relationships with some aspect of his environment as necessary for overcoming deviance, in the one case by removal of the offending Wind through ceremonial means and in the other case by such means as manipulating the consquences of the deviant behaviors (Mischel 1968:165). In accounting for behavior, both theories also give overt recognition to the effect of social influences upon the individual's behavior, conceptualized in both instances in terms of the efficacy of others' examples and of persuasive communications informing the individual of the likely consequences of particular behaviors (Mischel 1968:150–168; also see p. 39). Seen in this perspective, the Navajo emphasis on external determinants of thought and behavior, however alien to our way of thinking may be the code in which the basic message is conveyed, does apparently grasp a reality that our modern science has only recently begun to fully appreciate.

It is easy to overstate this argument. There are, of course, fundamental and critical differences between the Navajo theory and such theories as Mischel's. The theoretical relevance of Holy People, Messenger Winds, Ghosts, and witchcraft in Navajo explanations of behavior, and ceremonial practices for invoking beneficent spiritual agencies and exorcising harmful ones in Navajo prescriptions for behavioral change, are only a few of the features of Navajo belief which obviously diverge from anything proposed by social behavior theorists. Despite these qualifications, it must be recognized that physicians and psychiatrists personally attest to the therapeutic benefits of Navajo healing practices in some instances; and, as Horton has indicated, traditional theories may arrive at some reality-based causal connections, such as the relationship of sickness to disturbances of social life, prior to their full appreciation by modern science (Horton 1967:55–57).

SUGGESTIONS FOR FUTURE RESEARCH

There are a number of questions raised by the research described in the previous pages, the answers to which will depend upon future research efforts of other investigators.

One apparent need is to study the relationships between Navajo beliefs about the determinants of behavior and actual on-the-ground behavior; that is, what is the functional significance of these beliefs for Navajo behavior? Since the beliefs and concepts explored in the present study were elicited solely in formal interview situations, supplemental sociolinguistic studies should be made to determine their use by the Navajo in accounting for day-to-day behavioral events.

A second area of needed research in the light of the present findings relates to Navajo morality. If the Holy People are indeed conceived to be moral authorities, as is asserted here, there is a need for more specific information about the moral code attributed to them. Which aspects of Navajo morality derive from the Holy People, and which might be based solely on the pragmatic considerations emphasized by Ladd (1957)? This points to the need for a thorough reassessment of Navajo morality. Ladd's study has been subject to criticism for its reliance on the interviewing of a single informant, but it has nevertheless been very influential in supporting the prevailing view that Navajo deities are not involved in morality. Ladd's view, and that presented here, would be confirmed or refuted by further study. Confirmation of a moral component to Navajo religion would have several implications, not the least of which would be to help buttress Navajo religion against the onslaught of those who may take offense at the alleged amorality of Navajo religion. In addition, there is a need to further explore the effectiveness of supernatural sanctions in promoting Navajo conformity to ethical norms. The implication of religious changes for personal conduct and social interactions should also not be overlooked.

A third area for further research relates to the broader cultural context of the Wind concept. It would be informative to examine the belief systems of other Athabaskan-speaking groups, and also of the Puebloan groups that have influenced Navajo culture, in order to determine whether this concept is rooted in either or both of these traditions. It should also be noted that there are evidences of similarities of the Navajo Wind concept with the Dakota concept of Skan, "the Great Spirit" (Walker 1917), suggesting that the Navajo Wind concept may be a variant of a pan-Indian concept having a wide distribution among native North Americans.

ᴀᴘᴘᴇɴᴅɪx

Navajo Texts

The Navajo texts in this section are comprised of selected portions of the utterances of the cultural informants for this study, with interlinear translations in English. Each segment is referenced to numbered citations following English language free translations appearing throughout pages 9–48. The initials of the informant who was the source of each text element are given in parentheses following his transcribed statement.

1. Díí nahosdzáán ńléí hodideezlį́į́dą́ą́' ha'át'éego shį́į ts'ídá
   This Earth   when it started to   somehow very much
                                    exist

kót'éego niłch'i átsé hólǫ́ǫ́ la jiní. Áádóó diné nilį́į́go yaa
this way Wind first it   t.s.* From per- it   of
                        exists   there son being it

áhályą́ą́ lá jiní.
it takes   t.s.
care

---

*t.s. is an abbreviation that means 'they said' or 'it is said.'

Chahałheeł kót'éego ałk'idahsiláago kwe'é hosiidlíí', kwe'é
Darkness   like this   each other on   here   we started here
                         top lying   existing,

hazlíí' jiní. Kwe'é díí bikáá' dahsiláháá nít'éé' hayooł kááł
it hap-   t.s. Here this on top up it had lain   Dawn
pened

silíí'   jiní níléí gónaa hoogáhígíí.
it   t.s. that across whitening.
became

Ákohgo áadi díí   ałk'idahsiláháá nít'éé', nłch'i át'éélá
So   there these on one another it   Wind it is
                        lying   was,

jiní. Chahłeełyéę nít'éé'. Éí báá níléí chahałheeł níléí
t.s. Darkness   it was. That is that Darkness   that
                                       why

hakiildoh jó ł'ée'go da,   nizhónigo kót'éego dich'i. Díí át'éélá
settles   like at   when, beauti- in this   it   This it is
over you   night   fully   way   breezes.

jiní, diné át'éélá jiní. Nłéídéę' naaniiłkááh kót'éego nizhónigo
t.s., per- it is. t.s. From   when it   in this   beauti-
     son   there   dawns   way   fully

naaniidzígai yileehgo, dahsiláháá yikáítah, dich'i łeh   jiní.
across it   it   that   among the it   usual- t.s.
whitens   becomes, streak   Dawn   breezes ly

Nizhónigo nłch'i hólóólá jiní. Áadi níléidi ni'ł'áahdi   áadishíí
Beautiful- Wind exists   t.s. There back in the   there
     ly   there underworlds probably

ákohgoshíí díidí diné át'éélá jiní (J T).
so then it this per- it is   t.s.
  seems   son

2. Kót'éego bik'iidéél jiní áadi áádóóshíí índa dinétah hoolyéeji'
   In this onto it   t.s. back from there Navajo to the
   way   they passed   there   Land   place
                                                    called

dahadiidéél. Éí áádóó Saad Łá'í wolyéego, t'áá ła'í saad
they moved. From there Word One it is   just one word
                                   called,

ha'át'éegoshį́į́ bee yááti'go. Áádóó adeezdééł éí dibé
somehow   by being From   they   like
probably   it spoken. there moved   sheep

ádaat'éhígíígi át'éego. Jó dibé doo yáłti' da. Áko biná'ígíí
the way they it being. Sheep not they   So their eyes
are   Sheep not talk.

shíí t'éiyá yee naakai— kojigo dah diikáahgo, áajigo dah diijah.
it only by   they walk this if going to that they run
seems   them about— way they walk, way

Náánáá kojigo dó'. Ákót'éé ńt'ę́ę́' jiní. Doo saad t'éiyá ádin
Again this too. That way it   t.s. No words none
       way   was

jiní, áko t'óó da'hizhnil'į́ kot'éego. Ahiłdahojilne' dooleełígíí
t.s., so merely look at one this To each other to be
      another way.   one talks

adin. Akoo'dooleeł ha'níigo "wuuh, wuuh"ńdazhdi'niih jiní,
none. To   when they wish "whoo, whoo" they would t.s.,
      there to say   say

áko nizhónígo dazhdiits'a' jiní. Saad t'áá łá'í bee yááti'
so very well they under- t.s. Word One by he
       stand   it talks

yoolyéédę́ę́' jiní. Áádóó ńléí diyin dine'é danilį́igo ńléí,
it is called t.s. From then Holy People they being there,
from there   there

naaldloosh dine'é ts'ídá ałtso diné nilį́į́ lá jiní. Áádę́ę́'shį́į́
four-legged peo- abso- all people they t.s. From it
animals   ple lutely   are   there seems

átsé hastiin shį́į́ yáyiizį́', átsé asdzáán dó' yáyiizį́'.
First Man   it   stood for First Woman too for them
       seems them,   she stood.

   "Shí nihá eesh'į̄ doo" dííniid jiní. Áko ákót'éego nídiilyá
   "I for you I see will" he said t.s. So in this way it was
                    obtained

jiní, nłch'i Díí
t.s., Wind. This

átsé hastiin, átsé asdzáán dajoolyée ńléí haashch'éełt'í,
First Man,   First Woman the ones that Talking God,
              called

haashch'éóghaan, diné   dajíl̨įįgo, diyin dine'é dajíl̨įįgo, kót'éego
Calling God,   people they   Holy People they   in this
　　　　　　　　　　were,　　　　　　　being,　way

jookah. Nłch'i átsé hólǫ́ǫ́lá jiní, ákot'éego bik'ijiidéél   jiní
they   Wind first it   t.s., in that   they came upon t.s.
walked.   exists   way

diné nil̨įįlá jiní Ákohgoshį́į́ áádę́ę́, "Shee ééhózin dooleeł,
per- it was t.s. So it then from   "By me it is   will be,
son   seems   there,   known

shí! Nihí éí   doo nihił éédahózinda díí   k'ad dahdidoodiłgóó,
me! You that not with is known   this now where you will go,
　　　　　　　you

doo nihił bééhózinda" ní   jiní. "Shiłbééhózin łą́ą́" ní   jiní.
not with is known"   he t.s. "I   know"   defin- he t.s.
　you   said   itely" said

"Díí ts'ídá t'áá át'é shił bééhózin. Díí   nahosdzáán ts'ídá bii'
"This just every- with it is   This Earth   very in it
　　　　　thing me known.   much

nahazt'i dóó bikáá' nahaazt'i', ts'ídá ałtso shił bééhózin"
pathways and on it pathways, just all with known"
into it　　　　　　　　　　　　　　me

dííniid. "Shí éiyá nłch'i nishłí." Kót'éego áadi yee ahił
he said. "I   only Wind I am." In this   there   himself
　　　　　　　　　　　way   about

dahoolni'go. Áádóó bee iina silį́į́   jiní. "Ahéhee',   nídanihidoolá"
he told.   From by life it   t.s. "Thank you, you accepted
　　　　there him   became   us"

jiní.
t.s.

　　Kót'eégo ałk'i dah siláago áko díí   bik'ehgo dah adiildee'
　　In this they lying on so these accord- they started
　　way   one another   ingly   going

jiní. Chahałheełyę́ę́   dóó hayoołkáályę́ę́ dó', ákohgo díí   nłch'i
t.s. That which was and that which   too, so   these Winds
　　Darkness   was Dawn

silį́į́. Bee yéeji'ígíí nłch'i diłhił wolyée dooleeł. Ńléí
they   By was called Wind Dark it is   will be. There
became it   called

gónaa nahodeełʼiizh nahalingo kótʼéego hayoołkááł bił silá
across Sky Blue   it is like in this   Dawn   with it
                                   way   it   lies

nłchʼi dootłʼish wolyée dooleeł.
Wind Blue   it is   will be.
                called

Díí   nitsáhákeesyéé ńtʼéé́ ́ éi   nłchʼiyéé ńtʼéé́ ́ jó éí éí
This   the thinking   it was that Wind   it was so that
          of the past

saad silį́í́.   "Shí nihił   hashneʼ dooleeł" dííniid. "Haʼatʼéego
words it   "I   to you tell   will"   he said. "How
       became.

lá éí nihił johilneʼ dooleeł?" — áko díí nłchʼi éí jílį́,   ákohgo
that to us he tell   will?" —   so this Wind it he is, so

éiyá haayitʼée dooleeł?" "Tʼáá nihí   nihił béédahodooziił —
then now it   will be?" "Ourselves with it will be known —
                                     us

kʼad tʼóóshį́í nihił hashneʼ doo" náádooʼniid. Díį́ʼdí azlį́í,
now merely   to you I tell will   again he   Four it
     perhaps   be" said.   times happened,

tʼáádoo hołchʼííníʼą́ada   jiní. Kótʼéego "Nihił hashneʼ doo" —
not   to   he mentioned   t.s. This way "To you I tell will be" —
       them

éí doo n̋ı da.
that not he
    said.

Ákoshį́í́ áádóó dah adiildeeʼ, ńléí "ałnaashii dzideezdéél" wolyée
So it   from   they went   there "oppo-   they passed"   it is
  seems there   forth,   site   called

dooleeł. Kóneʼ   kodę́éʼ kótʼéego tó nílį́igo, áko ńléí dził
will be. Through from   like   water flow- so there mountains
         here   here   this   ing,

łichííʼgo naaznil jiní, tʼóó báhádzidígíí átʼé. Kéyah díí haz'ą́
being red are   t.s., very awesome   they Land this open
         located   are.

ńléí hónaanjí dóʼ, ákóhootʼé jiní, éí dził   kótʼéego niʼáh jiní
there across too, that's the t.s.,   moun- this   extend- t.s.
                   way it is   the tains way   ed

biyaa   góne' dó' ńléí halchíí' jiní. Tóhígíí dó' dinilchíi'go   nílį
under- to-   too it is red   t.s. The water too being red-
neath   ward there   dish flows

jiní. "Kǫǫayóó áhonoolnin lá. Kǫǫ́ kééhwiit'įį́ doo yooɫkááɫgóó"
t.s. "here   beautiful.   Here we live   will from now
        very much   be   on"

hodoo'niid. T'áá íídą́ą́' tsooz'įįd jiní: "Kwe'é nidoohdiɫ!"
it was said. Already   it was in   t.s.: "To this you will
                       use   point   move!"

kóne'   ho'doo'niid— ákoshį́į́ díí bijaa' díí kóne' beenásɫ'ah
through to them   so it this his   through earfold
here   it was said— seems   ear   here

ts'ídá doo hoot'įįda jiní. Kóne' nidiilniih doo na'iitsihgo
very   not it is seen t.s. In here we poke and poke it with
                            our fingers   something

da éí bééhózin jiní. Díí kóne' hóló jiní. Áádę́ę́ hach'į́'
when is known t.s. This in   it   t.s. From towards
that   here exists   there them

haadzíí' jiní. "T'áá kǫ́ǫ́nidoohdiɫ" hodoo'niid. "T'áá kwe'é." (J T)
it   t.s. "Right here you   to them it   "Right here."
speaks   settle"   was said.

3. "T'áá la'aaníí áníí la, díí ání!" Áádóó ńléí ts'ídá t'áá
   "It's really what he this he   From then just as
    true   said,   said!" there

hanádzihígíí   bikéé' kót'eégo hodideeshzhiizh jiní, nɫch'iígíí.
what he spoke its   that way it began hap-   t.s., the Wind.
          being   pening

Kǫǫ́ nídajiizdéél díí, ákohgo áadishį́į́ índa nida'iizdéelgo t'ah
Here they settled these, so   there it and having settled sud-
                       then   seems   there

ńt'éé' kodę́ę́' hanáá'oodzíí' jiní: "Naat'áanii éiyá la'
denly from again it was   t.s.: "A leader that one
       here spoken

ádadoohɫííɫ" hodoo'niid jiní. "Ts'ídá aɫą́ąji' kót'eégo dahsidáa
you will   to them it t.s. "Just   first in this   he sit
make"   was said   way

dooleeł, naat'áanii. Éí biiyaa kééhoot'įį dooleeł nihásizįįgo,
will be,   the leader. He under you live   will be for you he
                him   standing,

áko éí nihinanit'a'á   dooleeł. Kót'éego éiyá haasht'e' nidoohkah,"
so he your continu- will be. In this way orderly   you will
         ous leader   walk,"

hodoo'niid.
to them it
was said.

    Asdzání nílį̨įgo t'óó báhádzidgo, jóła' ákódaat'é. Díí
    Women being very, feared,   some are that These
                      way.

kóoní   asdzání ayóo naat'áanii, ádadil'į háágóóshį́į yáádaałti'
round   women strong leaders,   they act strongly   they speak
here   out

ákót'éhígíí hóló̧ jiní, "asdzá̧á̧ naat'ááh" wolyéego. "Díí
this kind   there t.s., "woman leader"   was called. "This
              was

kodę́ę́' kót'éego ha'oodzíí', haa'í shą' bił   hodoonih éidí asdzáán?
from   in this   it was   let's   with it will   that woman?
here   way   spoken,   her be told

Ha'at'íilá ní   dooleeł lá?" Áadi ńléidi asdzáányę́ę, "Hágo!"
What   she will be?"   Back there that woman, "Come!"
          say

bi'doo'niid, bił hóone'e: "Díí   kodę́ę́' kóshi'doo'niid ńléidi
to her it   to it was   "This from   I was told thus back
was said,   her told: here   there

éí bee nihá nihoot'á̧ chahałheeł ałnáozt'i' hoolyéedi kodi
it for us was planned Darkness Crosses   at the place
                                          called

nↄↄↄch'i dine'é bik'i'iidééł áko áadi yee nihá nihoní'á̧, 'T'áá
'Wind' Peo- upon them so there by for he   'Only
      ple   we happened   it   us planned,

shí, shik'ehgo dooleeł' ní. Díí k'ad éí kót'é" bi'doo'niid.
me, according it   he This now is this to her it
     to me   will be' said. way"   was said.

Ákohgo, "Lá̧'a̧a̧, t'áá aaníí sha'áłchíní, t'áá aaníí jiní.
So then, "That's it   my children, it's true t.s.
          right,   is true

Ákonihi'doo'niid áádóó nihii'   siláh   áádóó nihił halne'.
This to us it   then   within is   then   to us it
was spoken   us   placed   informs.

Nihinitsékees nilį."
Our thinking it is."

Áko éí biniinaa k'ad éiyá   bik'ehgo dooleeł, kódzaa   jiní.
So   it for that now it   according to will   it hap-   t.s.
    reason   (him)   be,   pened so

Áko aadóó naat'ááh niilyá wolyéi hazlįį'   jiní: "Naat'ááh
So   from   leadership was what is came   t.s.   "Leadership
    there   formed called   to being

wolyéi nidoolyééł, yáti'   wolyé nidoolyééł. Hóló̜, kodi hóló̜.
what is will be   speak-   called will be   It   now it
called   placed,   ing   placed   exists,   exists.

Bee naat'ááh nidoolyéełii daats'í   nihił béédahózin? Bee
By it leader-   will be   perhaps with are known?   By
    ship   placed   you   which

yádootihii   daats'í nihił béédahózin?"   nááhodoo'niid jiní.
words to be maybe by   are known?"   again it was   t.s.
    spoken   you   said

"Kodi nihił   béédahózin lá!"   "Hágoshįį, k'ad dooleeł."   Áadi
"This with is known!"   "Alright,   now it will   Then
    us   be."

naat'ááh niilyá   jiní, ńléidi.
leader-   was   t.s., back
    ship   formed   then.

Kóó naat'ááh nináádaahya'. Díí   bee   yádaati' dooleełii
Here leader-   again was   These by   they   will be
    ship   placed.   them speak

azaanaast'áán wolyéi   bee   yádootihii, díí   kó̜ó̜ nidaahya'. Kodę́ę́'
threatening   the ones   by   will be   these here were   From
words   called   them spoken,   placed.   here

áníigo éí bik'ehgo "Kót'éego ádadoołííł," níigo,   "áko doo
one   that by his "This way you will   he   "so no
saying   will   do,"   saying,

adziih da—díí t'áá   háni' bik'eh, t'áá íiznízinígíí   éí doo da."
mistakes—this your own   by it,   just the way you   that not."
    mind   want

Kót'éego íldee' jiní. Áadi shį́į́ kót'éego bee naat'ááh niilyá,
This way they t.s. There it that way by leadership was
  followed   seems   it   formed,

kodę́ę́' nłch'i yee hoł halni'go Haashch'ééłti'í jiłíinii (J T).
from Wind about to tell- Talking God the one
here   it   him ing   who is.

4. Íídą́ą́' t'áá díí ahil ndahwiilne'ígíí át'éego t'óó hoł
  Back like this each we are that way just to
  then   other telling   them

halne'go, "Kónáádíí'nííł, kónáádoohnííł," ho'di'nííigo. Jó t'áá
being told, "You should you two should being told So it is
         do this,   do this,"   thusly.

aaníí hoł halne' ńt'ę́ę́'. Bik'eh joo'ash ńt'ę́ę́ (J D).
true to he it By it they it was.
  them told was.   lived

5. "Nłch'i diłhił, nłch'i dootł'izh, nłch'i łitso, nłch'i
  "Wind Dark, Wind Blue, Wind Yellow, Wind

łigai, nłch'i disǫs k'ad díí bik'ehgo ádík'eh yéilti' dooleeł"
White Wind glit- now these by by their we will be"
       tering   them   will   speak

k'ad kódzaa jiní. T'áá éí bik'ehgo nanihik'í yáłti'ii t'áá
now like this So, accordingly, in our one who from
  happened t.s.   behalf   speaks

ńléídę́ę́' nihooshk'iizh dadeeskai. Éí t'áá éí nłch'i, t'áá éí
back then alongside us has been These same Winds, same ones
           present.

nanihik'í yádeiłtééh dóó áádę́ę́' danihiicheii ni' nanihik'í
for us they speak and from our ances- late in our
          there   tors   behalf

yádeiłtééhgo éí ánáádayiidlaa. T'áá áádę́ę́' nihinanit'á'í'
speaking it they made. From there our leader

nanihik'í yáłti'ii t'áá áádę́ę́' nihaa ádaahalyáanii bik'ehgo
for us who speaks from that for us ones who by them
            time   guide us

áádę́ę́' deiíléhígíí, éí díí jíídi k'ad ákót'é. Jó áadi
from they kept that this day now is like At that
there for us,   that. time

ákódanihilní éíbik'ehgo naniideeh (C A B).
they told us   according   we live.
   so   to them

6. Kodi n#ch'i nihaa ádahalyá dooleeł hidee'naadóó nihaa
   Now Winds of us they take will   from begin- of us
               care of   be   ning of life

áhályá dooleeł, éíkodi t'óó nihaa ádahalyá. Éíshį́į́ bik'ehgo
it takes will   that now   of us they take That   by it
care   be,   merely   care.

ahaa ádahwiilyá yoołkáátgóó   (C A B).
each we take   from now on.
other care

7. Díí nahosdzáán wolyéi biih hóole' índída naaki t'áá ałk'i
   This Earth   the one in it   and   two   one
             called her formed   another

dah sinil biih hóole', áko kodi yee nihá dah yists'id. Jó
on lying in formed, so here by for were put up. So
       her   it us

áko la ha'a'aahjį' áájígo nées'á, díík'ad nahosdzáánígíí, jó áko
then towards   in that she   this here Earth,   so
     east   way   faces,

ńláhjí aná'át'áhíjí áájí dées'eez.   Áko ńláh bizaad látah
over   where the Sun her feet   So   there her   fore-
there   goes down   are placed.   word most

áádóó yee haadzíí'. "Yidiiskáágóó shik'ih ndaahłizh índa
from   by she   "From now on on me you will   and
there   it   spoke.   urinate

shik'ih ndaahchį' índa bíighahági ádashoł'į́ doo índa yáadi
on me   you will   and whatever you do   will and things
    defecate   to me

nchǫ́'ígíí shik'įįį' kódaał'į́ dooleeł. Índa díí ádineeznáádóó
bad ones on me   you throw will.   And   when you die

t'áá kojį' ni'   t'áájį' náádleeł dooleeł. Doo háájí ndahohłeeh
just to   Earth to   back you go will. Not wherever you go
  here   there

da dooleeł."
will be."

"Díí   shiih yilyáago bee   haasdzíí'ígíí k'ad éí doo ninée da
"This placed inside by   I spoke   now that not die
        me   which

dooleeł— éí bee iináanii díí k'ad ałk'i dah sinilígíí"   ní   jiní.
will—   that by they   this now lying on one another" she t.s.
        it live   said

"Díí ałtsé shiih   yilyáhígíí éí diyin át'ee dooleeł, éí na'iiłnáá
"This first inside of me   that holy is will be, that move us
        placed

dooleeł, éí bik'ehgo kééhwiit'į̃ dooleeł yidiiską́ą́góó" ní   jiní.
will,   that by it we live   will   from here on" she t.s.
                                                              said

"Áádóó kodi índa bee hááhółyį́įh dooleełii   k'ad nihą́ąh
"And   here by it we rest   the one   now on you
                                 that will be

anáádoolníłʼ" kódzaa jiní. Áadi índa ńlááhjį́'   háá'át'áahjį̃'
also will put" hap-   t.s. There next towards to the east
              pened   there

bitsiit'áád alááhgóó ádaalne' dah didiilnii' díí éí nihináts'iin
on top of farthest sent   out her hand this our eyebrows
her head

kodóó yídeesnii' jiní. Kojí nááná kodóó ńt'éé' díí disho silį́į
from she   t.s. Over again from it   this nap   formed
here touched   here   here was

jiní. "Bił díí bee hááhółyį́įh dooleeł biłígíí éí k'ad" ákódzaa
t.s. "Sleep it by rest   will be that   now" happened
        means of   sleep

jiní. Áadi índa t'áá ha'a'aahjį̃' dah náádidiilnii'. Nihíchį́įh
t.s. There then to the east   again she reached Our nose
                                                    out.

kodę́ę́' díí nihináts'iin ałch'į̃' ndeelnii' yę́ędę́ę́' áádę́ę́' nihíchį́įh
from   this our eyebrows to- from where her from   our nose
here   gether fingers met   there

yaah dideesnii' koji' nihíchííh bílátahji'. "Díí éí ntsáhákees
she ran her   to   our nose to the tip. "This thinking
        finger here

át'ee dooleeł, díí éí bee nitsóhkees dooleeł" nihidííniid jiní.
it   will be, this by it you think   will" to us it   t.s.
                                                      was said.

"Ńlááh ha'a'aahjí áájí ńléí nahosdzáán biih   yilyáhę́ę́ áájí
"There in the east   that Earth   inside was   there
                        her   put

hólǫ́ǫ́ dooleeł, éi   saad ła'i   wolyée dooleeł. Kojí yę́ę́ bik'eh
it   will,   that Word One called will be.   This   *bik'eh*
exist   side

hózhǫ́ nlínę́ę   áájí   shádá'áahjí kodi áájí éiyá saad naaki
hózhǫ́ it was   there south side   there   Word Two

dooleeł" ní   jiní. "Kodóó índa naaki t'óó nihóoltą́' dooleeł,
will be" she t.s. "From   next two merely with you will be,
        said   here

éí t'oo bił ałta' sinil dooleeł: E'e'aahjí éí   saad táá'   dooleeł,
that just between placed will be: In the   there Word Three will
                                        west   be,

kojí náhookosjí. Áko saad díí'   alą́ą́jį' nanideeh dooleeł"
This in the   So   words four leading placed   will be"
side north.

hodoo'niid jiní. Díík'ad saad ła'ígíí jó 'diyinayói át'é, éí bi'áadii át'é.
it was said t.s. This   Word One   holy   very it   it female is.
                                                        is,

Áko   bikéé' gone'é biką'ii,   náá bi'áadii,   náá biką'ii, áko díí'
Then afterward   male one,   again female again male   so four
                                one,   one,

naandeeh (C A B).
grouped.

8. T'áá éí át'é. Díík'ad t'áá   yiidlą́ą́góó ts'ídá   t'áá ákót'éego
The same it This now when we keep   exactly in that way
        is.   increasing

nihii'heelye'. Áko diyingo bee ha'oodzíí', áko éí diyin kojí   ndi
within it is   It is holy   what was   that holy   on   but
us   put.   spoken,   this side

t'áá ákót'é. Díí saad biką'ii   nihigáál—t'áá nłch'i   t'áá éí
it is the   This Word the male our   Wind   the same
    same   one   gait—   one

nihigáál, éí bee   needáh. Díí kón'é saad táá' góne'ígíí
our gait, that by we   This next Word Three the next
        it   walk.   one

nihinitsékees,   ák'itsíndíílkosii   ádínidiit'áałii   na'ák'iyéilti'
our thinking,   for ourselves we   for ourselves   for ourselves
          think   we plan   we talk

dooleełii éí át'é.   Ádích'óhosiit'ą́ądi bik'ehgo deedzáadi
will be   that it For ourselves we   according when we
the one   is.   plan   to that   go

éí éiyá áadi   saad díį́'.   Jó áko kóy'éego ít'é.
that   there Word Four.   So in that way it is.

   Nłch'i nihigáál daazlíí'   índa nihiyi'   hazlį́į'   jó éí nihigáál
   Wind our gait became   and within us   it   so it our gait
                             formed

daazlíí'.   Dóó nłch'i t'áá éí nihiyi' náánéizi' lá, álílee naa-
became.   Then Wind same within again it   supernatur-
               one   us   stood,   ally

gháago.   Kóne'é yikáá' góne' t'óó biniit'aahjį' ánáánát'é. Jó
moving.   Next   on it   just next to it   again it is.

t'áá aheełt'éé lá jiní.   Eidí   bik'eh hózhǫ́ áko ałk'i dah
They are alike   t.s.   That *bik'eh hózhǫ́*   on each other

sinilgo jó kót'éego nihizaad....   Ákohgo índa jó k'ad
lying   so in that   our words....   So then   this
      way

"Éiyá nílááhdę́ę́' nanihiłnáa dooleełii hólǫ́ǫ doo" kódzaa jiní (C A B).
"That from there it moves   the one   exists will" hap-   t.s.
       us   will be   pened

9. Nłch'i níléí wóyahdi áadi niilts'id   áádę́ę́' ádeezná jó daaní.
   Winds there under   it formed from   they   this they
        it   there emerged   say.

Nłch'i kodóó díí k'os nineel'ą́ą́ dóó biyi'dóó naaki jiní. Níléí
Winds from   this cloud the ends from in from two t.s. There
   here   them

ni'   bitł'ááhdę́ę́' níléí ni'   bikétł'óól nikdiit'i'dę́ę́', tó bi-
Earth its from   there Earth its   from where it   water its
   bottom   roots   penetrates,

kétł'óól nikidiit'i'dę́ę́' naaki jiní. Áko shį́į́   ahidiniidee'
roots   from where it two t.s. Then it   they came
   penetrates   seems together

áádóó índa nílch'i ádééyi'nil jiní. Ts'ídá   hastą́ą́h silį́į́'
and then   Winds mixed up t.s.   Exactly six   it came
                                                       to

wódahjí, wóyahjí dó' hastą́ą́h jiní, áko naakits'áadah. Ákót'éego
above,   below   too six   t.s., so   twelve.   In that
                                                               way

ni'   bikáá' hazlį́į́'. Ákót'éego alkee' ninídee', bita'góne'
Earth on   it   In this   they fell in   between
        it   formed. way   order,   them

honiidlį́ díí ńléí bíla'ashdla'   nináneel'ą́ą́jį'. Díí nłch'iígíí
we   these human beings all of them.   These Winds
live

kojí hastą́ą́h; hóyahjí dó' hastą́ą́h, kojí ni'jí dó; hastą́ą́h;
over six;   below   too six,   over Earth's 'six,
here   here side   also

áko bita'góne' honiidlį́įgo. T'áá ałtso nihinaalnish. Díí
so   between them we live. All of them work on us. This

nłch'i nááyisii éí t'éiyá t'áá doo hózhǫ́ yá'át'éeh da jiní,
Wind Revolving   not very   good   t.s.,
                   that

índa nłch'i noots'ee' wolyéi eii doo yá'át'éeh da. Díidí
and Wind Coiled   called it   not good.   This

nłch'i noodǫ́ǫ́z... áko nááná, dį́į́'. Éí éí kwe'é ałtah
Wind Striped... and again, four. These here among

nahoo'níł jiní éí díí. Ńlááhjí ni'   nááyis, ńlááhjí wódahjí
different t.s. these. Over   Earth re-   over   above
things happen   there   volves, there

yá náayis k'ad kót'é, áko bita'gi honiidlį́įgo kwe'é. Áko
Sky revolves like this, so between we live   here.   So

kodę́ę́' naałniih náhoodleeł. Kót'éego éiyá ninihi'deelyá   jiní,
from problems increase.   In this   we were placed t.s.,
this   way

díí bíla'ashdla' nináneel'ą́ą́jį'. Áko t'áá alts'ą́ą́hjí bą́ąhígóó
these humans all of them.   So   on both sides bad things

áhooníł t'áá ałts'ą́ą́jí bą́ąh dahist'ą́ jini (C A B).
happen both sides on   were   t.s.
            them placed

10. Nłch'i éí t'áá łá'i   ákondi ashdla' bee wóji— nłch'i
Wind   that just one but   five   by it is   Wind
                                  it   called—

diłhił, nłch'i dootł'izh, nłch'i łitso,   nłch'i łigai,   nłch'i
Dark,   Wind Blue,   Wind Yellow, Wind White,   Wind

disǫs,   nłch'i   biyázhí (G E S).
Glossy, Wind's Child.

11. Dził   bii'   da'iilzi'yéé éí shíí   kodóó nihidiyin nilįigo
Moun- with-   they   these it from   our sacred being
tains   in them stand   seems then

kodóó bee danihi'dééji' nihidiyin.   Ńlááhjí diyin nilįinii
from   by to our end   our sacred. Over   Holy the One
then   them   there   that is

ánihiilaayę́ę kodóó índa diyin.   "Bee hinonáa doo"   nihíhígíí ní
the One that from   then sacred. "By   you live will"   ours said
    made us   them

jiní. Éí díí dził   bii'   da'iilzi', sisnaajiní, tsoodził,
t.s. These moun- with- they   Mt. Blanca, Mt. Taylor,
       tains   in   stand,

dook'o'oosłííd, dibé ntsaa, dził ná'oodiłii, ch'óol'į́'į́   (C A B).
San Francisco Hesperus   Mt. Huerfano, Gobernador
Peaks,   Mountain,   Knob.

12. Áko kwii hayoołkááł asdzą́ą́ hayoołkááł hastiin bił ts'aa'
So   here Dawn   Woman Dawn   Man   with basket
ńlááhgóó niinínil   índída dzą́ądi yiiyaa inílaagi t'áá éí
right   placed it and   here beneath placed   the same
there   it

hayoołkááł biyaa niilkaad,   bikáa'gi t'áá hayoołkááł. Nahodeetł'izh
Dawn   beneath was   on top   the Dawn.   Sky Blue
        it   spread,   of it

biyaa niilkaad,   nahodootł'izh bi'áadii díí hayoołkááł biiyaa.
beneath was   Sky Blue   Female this Dawn   under-
it   spread,   neath.

Hayoołkááł asdzą́ą́, hayoołkááł hastiin, nahodeetł'iizh asdzą́ą́,
Dawn   Woman, Dawn   Man,   Sky Blue   Woman,

nahodeełʼiizh hastiin, nahotsoi asdzą́ą́, nahotsoi hastiin, áko
Sky Blue   Man,   Twilight Woman, Twilight Man,   so

dii biyaa ńdaaskaad. Dibé lá, lííʼ la, nłʼiz lá, díí biyaa
these be- were   Sheep, horses, jewels, this under
neath it spread.   them

ńdaaskaad tsʼaa biiʼ naaznilgo, goʼídaalya   (C M).
were   basket in being   like that they
spread   it   placed,   were made.

13. Áádóó índa kodóó hózhǫ́ǫ́jí yichʼiʼ hadeʼdeezʼą́. Tʼáá ląish
    And from then Bless-   to-   they sang.   Not many
    then   ingway   wards it

nihideestʼą́, tʼáá díį́ʼį hahideestʼą́, ńláahdi tsʼídí bee
they sang, just four were sung,   back then really by
                                                    it

daʼiiznáaʼii. Áko díí biyaa   niiłkaad dóó łaʼ bikáaʼgi
they moved So   these under spread and some on top
the ones.   them

ndaaskaadę́ę́: Jó nahodeełʼiizh asdzą́ą́,   hastiin, áko díí ałkʼi
were placed: Well Sky Blue   Woman,   Man,   these together

ńláah, áko kodi shíí   iłhąąhndaastʼįid; díí bikʼéhʼéstiʼgo   biyaadi
joined, and here it   one another   these being covered under
                        seems they bothered;   it

iłhaahndaastʼįid. Kodi biyaadi daʼdiiznáá, díí   ikáájíyę́ę́ ła
one another they Here under   movement these that   some
bothered.   them   began,   were spread

íyaa diskaad łaʼ bikáʼii   sikaad. Kweʼé biyaa daʼidéél.
underneath some male spread. Here   under something
    spread   ones   them formed.

Áko éí nłchʼi... dząądi iih   haleehii... éí átʼé   (C M).
So that Wind... here enters the one   that it is.
           (us)   that forms. . . .

14. Jó díí asdzání bił   haanihitʼaashgo áko ńlááhdę́ę́ tsʼíítooʼ
    So this girl with having inter-   from there   bodily
                  her   course   fluids

ahihiʼidiilyéhídi   kodi awééʼ nihindéh. Áko áadi kojí diné
together join where   baby forms.   So there this manʼs
        here   side

ts'íítooí áádéé' nłch'i yee hinánéé la   áádéé' asdzání yee
bodily from   Wind by he   one from the   by
fluid   there   it   lived   there girl   it

hinánéé dó' la' áádéé'. Áko t'áá'aaníí naaki át'é. Jó áá
she   too one from   So really   two   there So there
lived   there.   are.

atsániitł'ishéé bii' hólónígíí éí díí k'ad áadi "sá'áh naagháí"
where it formed in   the one that now there "sá'áh naagháí"
him existing

diłní, "bik'eh hózhǫ" diłní (C M).
they 'bik'eh hózhǫ" they
call it   call it.

15. Kodóó yá'át'éehgo
    From   well
    here

baa nitsííkeesgo— áko jółíí' da bee hinii'náa leh,   béégashii
about when we those horses by we live usually, cattle
them think—   them

da tł'ízí da t'áá ałtso   bee   iináá shíí— nłch'i bee bił ééhózin
and goats and every- by   we   Wind by they know
        thing which live—   it

jiní. Éí bee   bił ééhózin jiní. Nihinitsékees bił bééhózin jiní (C A B).
t.s. That by they know t.s. Our thinking they know   t.s.
        it

16. Jó diné díidí nłch'i diyin nilíinii bik'eh hózhǫ nilíinii
    So Peo- these Wind Holy the one bik'eh hózhǫ the one
    ple

éí ákǫǫ naazh'áázh. Jó éí naadą́ą́' néiníjaa' jo   nídishní. Bichiin
these to they   That corn they brought to you I Her epi-
there went.   back   say.   dermis

do' díí áájí dah sidáii asdzáán nádleehé bichiin. Éidí éí baa
too this over who sits Woman Changing her epi- That they of
        there   dermis.   it

áhályą́ągo naadą́ą́' neest'ą́ áko.... Bitádídínéé éí bąąh nanool-
taking   corn   it   so.... Its pollen that from they
care   ripened   it

dee'. Éí kodóó éí diné bit'aalyá jiní. Éí bąąh ályaa jiní.
ga-   That then people was put t.s. That on was   t.s.
thered.   in them   them   put

Áko díí naadą́ą́' łigai yéę aháájaa'. Hashtł'ishnii ła' ánályaa
Then this corn white that was   Mud People one was made
                    was divided.   again

jiní, ła' kiiyaa'áanii áko. Naadą́'ą́łtsoii yéę ahánáánájaa'.
t.s., one Tall House also. Corn yellow that again was
          People   was divided.

Éí tódích'íi'nii áko, tó'áhaní bił ánáánályaa.... Kodóó
These Bitter Water Near Wa- with again were   From
       People,   ter People made....   here

t'óó nídidoo'nahígo ádaho'diilyaa   jiní. "T'áá azee' bił ánáá-
just he will be   they were made t.s. "Medicine with again
    getting up

dooníł" hodoo'niid jiní. Áádóó índa díí   tádídínę́ę nanooldee'
will be it was said t.s. And   this corn pol- was scat-
made"   then   len   tered

yéę éí nihąąh ályaa jiní t'áá át'é.... Díí asdzáán nádleehé
that on us was t.s. all of it.... This Woman Changing
was   put

bich'i' nijizh'áázh yéę nłch'i diłhił, nłch'i dootł'izh bił
to her the two went Wind Dark, Wind Blue, with

ákohgo, "T'áá nihí ákǫ́ǫ́ nishoo'ázhígíí t'áá ni biyi'góne' andi'-
this "You two to you who went just you within you
way,   there   them

doolyeeł, ni dó'. Ákohgo ałk'i dah siláago éí bee yáłti' doo"
be put, you too. This one lying on the that by you will"
              way   other   it talk

hodoo'niid. "Lą́'ąą" nááhodoo'niid. Ńléí góyaa nihizh'áázh yéę
it was said. "Al- again it was There down the two went past
        right"   said.

ńt'ę́ę́' t'áá eii biih hojíile' jiní (C A B).
it was these in them they t.s.
              went

17. Są'ąh naaghái wolyéi bik'eh hózhǫ́ wolyéi, t'aa éí nihii'
    Są'ąh naahgáíí the *bik'eh hózhǫ* the   this within
              one called   one called, us

sizí kodi. Éí ídahnihiila, éí nihá   yádaałti',   t'áá éí nihii'
it   here.   They made us, they for speak,   the same in
stands   us   us

hóole' (C M).
exist.

18. Jó t'áá táá'gi daats'í díí'   daats'í éí daats'í   t'áá ííyisíí
    Well   three perhaps four perhaps these per- really
                                                   haps

diné bidziil niha dadées'eez. Díí nahosdzáán jó áko díí éiyá
people strong for their feet This Earth   well that
                    us   are planted.

ts'ídá asdzáá   hwǫǫyaanii shíí át'é, ts'ídá t'áá altso dah
abso- woman wise one   it   she is, just everything she
lutely   seems

yooléél nídídzih nináaneel'ąąjí'. Áko kojí nahasdzáán yee
owns   breathes to the last one. Over here Earth   by it

ńdidziihii bii' hólónii ts'ídá shíí   bidziilii bii' hólǫ́.
she breathes in existing abso- it   strong   in   exists.
           her   lutely seems one   her

Ńlááhjí yádiłhił t'áá ákot'é (C M).
Over   Sky   it is the
there   same.

19. Kojí hayoołkááł hastiin, nahodeełʼiizh asdzáá,
    Over Dawn   Man, Sky Blue   Woman,
    here

kojí nahotsoi hastiin, kojí hayoołkááł asdzáá.
over Twilight Man,   over Dawn   Woman.
here   here

Áko éí nitsíí'iłkees. Éí   bik'ehgo nitsíí'iłkees.
So these make us think. According we think.
                      to them

    Éí t'óó tsohodeeskééz índa ńléídę́ę́' índa tsohodeeskéézígíí
    That just beginning then from   then that beginning of
          of thinking   there   thinking

éí chalhałheeł yimąs. Jó éí éí hayoołkaał ashkii bikéédę́ę́'
that Darkness Rolling. So that Dawn   Boy   after it

ńlááhdę́ę́' hayooɬkááɬ ashkii ńláahdi heeɬkááhgo jó áko.   Áaji'
from there Dawn   Boy   there   when it   you see. To
                                        dawns   there

háájílyigo áko ts'édzídzi' háágóóshį́į́ hatah yá'áhoot'éeh ɬeh
you rest   then you awaken   one's well   usually
                                        parts

hoɬ dah hózhǫ́ǫ leh. Ńléídę́ę́' ha'oo'áaɬgo jó éí sháándíín,
with   well usually. From   when the Sun there sunlight,
you   then   is about to rise

kodę́ę́ díí nihi'dinídíín, áko yá'át'eehii bee nihi'dinídíín.
from   this on us shines, the good one   by on us shines.
here   it

Éí bee nitsí'iɬkees (C A B).
That by we think.
    it

20. Biyi'gi bąąhágii áhooníɬ díí chahaɬheeɬ. Ńlááhdę́ę́' doo
    Within evil   happens this Darkness. From there not
    it

ádahalyánígíí binɬch'i hólǫ́   (C A B).
wise ones   their Wind exists.

21. K'ad ɬa'   shį́į́ nichǫ́'ǫ́gíí shį́į́ ɬa' hąąh   naazį́ éí, jó éí ígíí
    Here some it   bad one   some   beside it   they
                       seems   them   stands,

doo hats'íí ńdaohoji'áah da nahalin, áko díí ts'ídá yá'át'éehii
not well   they plan   it seems, see this really good one

bii' sizíinii eida t'áá aɬtso   bąą   hólǫ́ ndi. Jó kodi ch'íní'áh
in   stands those everything on   exists   Here mentioned
them   them even.

nɬch'i t'áá aɬ'ąą át'é. Naaki nihitah hólǫ́, ɬa' yá'át'éehi hólǫ́,
Wind   different are. Two among us exist, one good one exists,

ɬa' nichǫ́'ǫ́gi hólǫ́. T'áá aɬ ąą bizhi' hólǫ́: Nɬch'i yá'át'éehii
one bad one exists. Different their are: Wind good one
                                  names

hayooɬkááɬ ashkii bee wóji; nɬch'i doo yá'át'áehii chahaɬheeɬ
Dawn   Boy   it is called; Wind not good one   Darkness

nɬch'i yimąsii   wolyé   (C M).
Wind Rolling One it is called.

22. Éí nayiłná, éí t'áá eii   neiyiłná. Ńlááhdę́ę́' binanit'á'í
These move these same move it. From there their
    it, ones leader

niljįnii t'óó ńléídę́ę́' sidá jiní. Ńléí háá'át'áhídę́ę́' ła',
the one from there he t.s. There from where one,
who is sits the Sun rises

kojí shádá'ááhdę́ę́' ła' jiní. Ła' nighéí aná'át'áhídę́ę́' jiní,
over from the one t.s. One over from where the t.s.,
here south there Sun sets

ła' nighéídę́ę́' jiní. Áko t'áá díį'dę́ę́'go áko éí kodi éí
one from over t.s. So from four ways these here these
    there

bik'ehgo jiní (C A B).
according t.s.
to them

23. Díí k'ad dził ahéénínil biyi'di jo áadi t'éiyá naat'áanii
These here moun- sur- within there leaders
    tains rounding them

daanilį. Ts'ídá ha'át'íida binaahjį' dahodooleeł yá'át'éehgo
are. Abso- anything against will exist being good
    lutely them

dooleeł, ts'ídá t'áá ałtso binaahjį' yidooltséeł. Jó éí kót'éego
will be, just everything against will be seen. So in this
    them way

díí dziłígíí bii' dah'iike'di éí ákót'é. Áko áádę́ę́' jó t'áá
these moun- in they were in that See from just like
    tains them placed way. there

bilagáana jí Wááshindoon dishnǫ́ǫ́—áádę́ę́' siláago yiisnil dishní.
white way Washington I say— from agents placed I say.
    there

Áko díí ńlááhdę́ę́'ígíí t'áá ákonáánáát'é dził bii' dah'iike'dę́ę́'
So these from there just like that moun- in placed
    the ones tains them from

áádę́ę́' nłch'i díí aláąji' naat'áanii danilíinii (C M).
from Winds these fore- leaders they are
there most the ones.

24. Doo ał'ąą át'ée da. T'áá łá'ígíí át'éego át'é. Díí
Not dif- they are. Just one that way it This
ferent is.

nihii' sizínígíí bee yéiilti'ii t'áá ła'ígíí át'éego át'é.
within which by we talk just one that way it is.
us stands which

Bits'ánídaazt'i'. Éí t'áá łá'ígíí át'ée ndi t'áá ał'ąą át'éego
It derives from It just one is but different being
them.

bee wójí (C A B).
by it is
which called.

25. T'áá shį́į́ dį́į́'í jó díí dinéjí éí dajiní hastoiyę́ę...
That it four so this Navajo it they older men
seems way say past...

nłch'i diłhił wolyé jiní, nłch'i dootł'izh wolyé jiní, nłch'i
Wind Dark it is t.s., Wind Blue it is t.s., Wind
called called

łitso wolyé jiní, nłch'i łigai wolyé jiní. Jó t'áá dį́į́'í
Yellow it is t.s., Wind White it is t.s. So four
called called

díí bee ńdiidzihii. Ałdó' t'áá łá'i bee ńdiidzi ndi díí'
these by we breathe. Also just one by we al- four
them it breathe though

bee ńdiidzih (H B).
by we breathe.
them

26. Awéé'ígíí jó ńláahdi niitłíishgo ákohgo kodóó t'áá íídą́ą́'
A baby over when it is so there already
there to be formed

biyi' łeh t'áá áłah t'áá ahóoltą'go jó t'áá ła'ígíí át'éego
in it usual- both connected so just one it being
ly together being

át'é. Koji' kodóó bahsi'áanii díí nihii' sizíinii díí álílee
it Here from the main this within standing *álílee*
is. here part us this

naagháii jó éí át′é, kodóó índa bik′eh hózhǫ kojí... (C A B).
naagháii that it from next *bik′eh hózhǫ* this
        is, here   side....

27. Jó álílee naagháii nanihiiłná.... Níłch′i áłt′íisi
   Well *ali- naagháii* moves   Wind Little
        lee   us....

wolyéi éí bik′eh hózhǫ át′é. Jó éí nanihiiłná,   jó éí bik′ehgo
the one it *bik′-* hózhǫ So that moves us, that accord-
called *eh*   it is.   ing to it

hinii′ná.... Jó kót′éego ałk′i dah sa′ą díí   álílee naagháii
we live.... So in this on each placed this *áli-*
        way other   *lee naagháii*

jó níłch′i kóne′é áłt′íisígíí akáá′ dah sa′ą díidí, jó áko
  Wind in   the little on   is placed this so then
    here   one top   one,

yéiilti′ (C A B).
we talk.

28. Jó bi′niitsąhdóó ts′ídá díí′ beeńdeedzidgóó ako ńláahdi
   Starting from exactly four months   there
   conception

bii′ sizínę́ę̨ dehkót′íí. Áko ńláahdi dehkót′įgo áko hiditnáh
in it   grows   There when it grows it moves
it stood upwards.   upwards.

.... Áko ńláahdi éí bii′ iideeł nahalin t′áá íídą́ą́′ bii′
.... So there that in it goes it seems already in it
        it

siláh kodi. Hazhó′ó kojį́′ yileehgo índa ákogo kót′į, hidi′nah.
placed here. Slowly to   coming   then this it moves.
        here to be   it does,

Jó kót′éego áádóó índa dee′áanił, dee′áanił, dee′áanił
So in this from it keeps growing, growing
    way there growing,

ts′ídá ńléí ídidoo′nahjį́′ ahaalzhish (C A B).
just there to where it that time.
        will be born

29. Ńléí ts'ídá yá'át'éehii   nłch'i éí ńlááhdę́ę́' yíneiyiilts'óód
    There abso- good the one Wind it from   it adds on to
       lutely   there   itself

índa bik'eh hózhóónígíí t'áá ákót'é (C A B).
and bik'eh hózhóónígíí   is the same
        the one   way.

30. Ła'   shį́į́ yá'át'éehgo ii' sizį́į́ shį́į́ iih   dayiiléh. Ła shį́į́
    Some it being good within it within it   Some it
    . seems   stands   places.   seems

t'áá shághaaníjį', ła' shį́į́ t'áá nahgóó hatsii' yidoogah
to so far,   some to there one's   will become
                               hair   white

danízin'ígíí hwiih dayiiléh. T'áá ał'ąą doo t'áá łá'ígíí da,
that they   within it   Different not just one,
think   one   places.

azhá shį́į́ ákónéíláá' ndahodiichíí shį́į́ ndi ał'ąą   át'ée hwiih
even though so many are born   but differ- it   within
                                         ent   is

dahalyé nahalin (J D).
are   it seems.
placed

31. Jó éí nihiyi'di éiyá díí k'ad   kodę́ę́' nihizéé' dóó kwííyah
    So this within this presently from our   from down
             us   here   mouth   here

jó kwííyah sizį́ nahalin. Éí bee ńdiidzih. Ts'ídá t'áá ałtso
see down it it   That by we   Just all
     here   stands seems.   it breathe.

nihi'ts'oos niyiiłnah, t'áá át'éé ńt'ę́ę́' nihitah niyiiłnáh.
our vessels it moves, all parts   our   it moves.
                                      bodies

Jó éí bee hinii'ná. Nihi'jéí ndi áadi jó éí t'áá át'é
So that by we live. Our heart even that it all
     it

niyiiłná (H B).
it moves.

32. Nłch'i dii bee hinii'ná nihí diné.   Áko ńléí itsądziztįh
   Wind this by we live we Navajo. When there one is in
       it   the womb.

ńléí hamá bitsądzizį t'áá jó ńléí kót'éego nłtsogo nahalingo
there one's in her   there this way at a cer- it seems
  mother womb   tain rate

honaał, honaał. Ńléidi ałtso hadaaniłt'eehgo jó áadi ńláahjí'
he de- he   There finished developing there to there
velops, develops.

ch'íhindéh. Áádóó índa jó éí bik'ehgo áádóó índa náástaghádóó
he falls   From   that accord- then   when he goes
  out.   then   ing to it   so far

ńléijį' yáłti' yileeh. Dzą nłch'iígíí
there he it comes   this Wind
     talks to be.   Then

éí yee hiniiyéego k'ad éí ńléí jó éí bik'ehgo jiní (H B).
that by growing   now that   that according t.s.
    it   to it

33. T'áá ániíltso nłch'i t'éí bee yéilti'.   Nihitsoo' bílátahgi
   Everybody Wind only by we talk. Our   at the tip
                     it   tongues

kwii danahale' (C M).
here they
   exist.

34. Díí k'ad nihíila' bílátahjí' hadatneests'ee' kǫǫ. Áko kojį'
   These here our at the tips there are   here. So here
         hands   spirals

nłch'i hadanees'ą. Díí nihiiké diní biníjį' t'áá ákót'é, áádóó
Winds stick out.   These our at our toes it is the   and
                  feet   same,

kǫǫ dahodit'ódígóó nihąą dahólǫǫgo át'é, díí nłch'iígíí ákǫǫ
here where soft   on us existing   they these Winds there
       parts   are,

adatneests'éé'go át'é. Nihiitsiit'áadi kodi jó áko deet'éí
being spirals   there Our head top of here you see certain
               are.

shį́į́ ałchíní naakigo hanoots'ee' łeh kodi, ła' éí   t'áá da
   children two   spirals   usually   some just
                    here,   they

łá'i jó áko kodi.   Áko éí níłch'i naaki yee dahináanii át'é
one you see here. So they Winds two   by they live   it is
                             them

dishní Díí koji'   hádaniists'éé' nihikélátahjį'yígíí nahosdzą́
I say. These here spirals   our toes at the   Earth
                           the tips'   ones

yinihółtą'. Nihilálátahjį'ígíí ńláahjį' yádiłhił yinihółta'.
hold us   Our fingers the   there   Sky   hold us to
to it.   at the tips   ones   it.

Áko éí bąą díí yiidáálgo doo naa'iigeeda (C M).
So these be-   when walking not we fall.
     cause of

35. Ńlááhdę́ę́' níłch'i áko éí k'ad níłch'i diyin wolyéi índa
    From there Wind   that now   *níłch'i diyin* the one and
                                    called

níłch'i álílee naagháii jó díí nihii'   sizį́. Áko díidí kad díí
níłch'i álílee naagháii so this with- it So this   same one
                         in us stands.

ńléi naagháii náayis dishní. Díí   náayis dishní. Tó náayis, t'áá
that one that it   I say. This it   I   Water it   every-
      walks turns   turns say.   turns,

ałtso. Áko éí nihidiyin éí t'éí át'é. Ts'ídá t'áá át'é
thing. So it our Holy alone it is. Really just it is
nihitsodizin t'éí át'é (C A B).
our prayer   only it is.

36. Níłch'i biyázhí wolyéi díí t'áá ńt'ę́ę́' tó nahalingo bii'
    Wind's Child the one this   water being in it
                called   like that

kééhwiit'į. T'áá éí nanihiłáh   níłch'iígíí.... Jó ákon
living.   Same one moves us this Wind.... You see

níłch'i biyázhí t'áá át'é nihitát'ah hóló̜, nihiyi'di hóló̜,
Wind's Child   same one within our it   within us it
                    tissues   exists,   exists,

nanihiłáh, nitsínihiiłkees   (G E S).
it moves us, it causes us to
     think.

37. Díí áájí   nłch'i diłhił   daanilííníí, nłch'i dooł'izh,
    These over Winds Dark   the ones   Winds Blue,
        there   that are,

nłch'iłitso   daanilį́, nłch'iłigai   daanilínígíí, éí áájí
Winds Yellow they   Winds White the ones   these over
        are,   that are,   there

t'áá át'é díí jį́į́góó   shį́į́   áájí   shį́į́   yił   hólǫ́. Áko kodi
all   this day to it   there it   with it   So   here
             seems   seems them exists.

bee'iikáahdi éí nłch'i t'óó   bee'iikáahgo sinilígíí áko
in sand-   these Winds when in sand-   placed   then
paintings   paintings

áájígo bijaa'at'ahii kwii t'áá ákót'éego, iikááh naazhjaa'
in that their ear-   here just like that,   sand- made
way   folds   paintings

t'áá bił dahalne'go Jó nihí t'óó bee   íl'įh   nahalinígíí, t'óó nihik'ijį'
talking to them.   See ours merely copy it seems,   towards us

hóolyah éí áájí kojí t'óó   bee'iikááhjí   éí ákót'éego (B Y).
it was   that over here in the way of   it is that
given   there   sandpaintings   way.

38. Éí bilagáana, t'áá ałtso nihídó', béésh halné'é t'áá áko
    The white   everyone we too, telephone   always
        man,

nízhdii'áhii, "uh huh, uh huh" jiníigo, ahił   ahwiizhniilnih
which one   "uh huh, uh huh" saying, each we say something
picks up,   other

ákót'é jiní. Nihídó' nłch'i hólǫ́ǫ́ ńt'éé' jiní. Éí shį́į́
that it t.s. We too Wind have used t.s. That it
   is   to   seems

bik'ehgo ahił   dahojilne' nihíjíyę́ę́ éí nihaa náádiilyá (J T).
being   each they talk   in our   it from back was
which   other   past way   us   taken.

39. Kwe'é nihąąh sizį́, níłch'i ałch'ishjí ła' nihąąh sizį́.
    Here along us it Wind on each one along stands.
            stands,   side   us

Áko éí díígíí éí   nihił halne', "Áádéé̖' nichǫ́'ǫ́go nitsékeeséé̖
So   these this us   tells,   "From evil way he thought
                                 there

sizį́   ninełʼį́" hałní nahalin. Áko éí ńláahjį' haatsitsííd   (C M).
he   looking they it   So they over there keep watch.
stands at you" say   seems.

40. Díí nihii' sizínígíí t'áá éí díí   kojį' hadanees'ą́ nahalin.
    This the one standing same one here sticks out it seems.
                within us

T'áá éí bee   ńdiidzih t'áá ałtsojį' jó daaní. T'áá éí nihii'
That one by we   everything that they Same one in us
       it breathe   say.

sizį́, níłch'i ałts'íísí. Ákǫ́ǫ́   ł'óódadiits'a'ígíí da éí shį́į́
it   Wind Little. Around the ones that   too that same
stands,   here   are sounding

t'áá éí biyi' dahólǫ́ t'áá át'é éí ákǫ́ǫ́.   Jó t'áá díí nihii
one in   they   all of those around Just this within
        them exist   here.   us

sizínígíí nihijaa't'ahjį' hadanees'ą́ díí kǫ́   nihílálátahjį'
it stands our earfolds it sticks   this here our finger-
                out   tips

da kojį' jó dajińígo baa   dahojilne' (B Y).
too to so they say about they talk.
  here   it

41. T'áá shį́į́ diyin shį́į́ áádéé̖' nihii'   dayiizla', nihidiyin
    That it   Holy   from within they were our Holy
        seems   there us   put,

daanilíinii.... Áádéé̖' ákót'éego áádóó ákǫ́ǫ́ nihitahgóó
the Ones   From in this   and around among us
that are....   there way   here

ńdayiizla' t'áá át'é   (B Y).
they were all of them.
  put

42. T'áá ałtso yá'át'éehii bił   nibi'diichííh (C A B).
    Every one a good one with he is born.
                 it

43. Jó kodę́ę́' ashiiké jilį́į́dą́ą́'   éí íníí' ádin,   áájí atisnłtso
 So from boys are when then thought is there it is
 here lacking, greater

nahalin. Áko dzą̧ą̧di hwii' sizínígíí ts'ídá shį́į yá'át'éehii
it sems. So then the one that really it is good
  stands within one

hwii' sizį́į̧go ndi áko kodę́ę́' t'áá doo daal'íinii ádajile'.
standing but then from misbehavior they make.
within one here

Áko áadi doo hóji̧ł'i̧hígíí ako áadi éíyę́ę̧ t'áá éí hoch'i̧'
So then wrong doing there that same one towards
  oneself

anááhonitin, t'áá hwí nabik'eh ndzídziłkeesgo.... Kwe'é
it teaches, oneself about it thinking.... Here

doo ákóójit'i̧héegi kwe'é nabik'eh tsídzíkeesgo kodę́ę́ hach'i̧'
wrong doing here about it thinking from towards
  here oneself

ch'éehyiiłkeed nahalin. Kodi hwii' sizínígíí éí ít'i̧: "Áko
it shows back it seems. Here the one that it does "So
  stands within it:

kwe'é hwiíndzaagi! Dooda! K'ad nínił'i̧!" hałní nahalin, díí
here what you did! No! Here you look it tells it these
  at it!" one seems,

doo ákóójit'i̧héegi. Áko áadi noosééł nahalin dzą̧ądi hayi'di
wrong doings. So there it grows it there within
  seems one

hanitsékees'ígíí, níłch'iígíí kodi hanáásnoosééł nahalin (C M).
one's thoughts this Wind here also grows it seems.

44. "Bíni' bidziil" daanínígíí éí ákót'éego ázhdiil'i̧h t'áá
 "His it is what they when it is one makes every-
  mind strong" say that way himself

ałtso níhónítahgo áko éí háni' bidziil áko yéego. Doo
thing when it then one's is very. Not
  tries one mind strong

akójít'i̧hgóó éiyá doo háni' níłdzil da háni' doo bidziil da
one does that then not one's is one's is not
  mind stable mind strong

hwii' sizíinii doo bidziil da.... Jó éidí ákót'éego
within one   not it is   So that in that
it stands   strong....   way

bee nahodintingo baa ákonízingo hojíyą́ągo áko díidí ts'ídá t'áá
by if one is   of   if one is   if one is   then this just every-
it taught   it   aware   wise

ałtso beezhnéł'į́ deeyikáhgóó ahilheed nahalin. Ákohgo bik'ehgo
thing by one   to where   it shows it seems. Then   according
       it looks they walk   to it

joogáał dóó bee nááhizdidziihii bidziilgo áko "Ńléiga' doo
one   and by one breathes   if it is then "That not
walks   it   strong

ál'íi da lá, doo ajił'į̨ da lá" t'áá ákwííjí hach'į́ ch'ííyiłheed
should   not you should everyday towards it flicks
be done,   do"   one

nahalin (C L).
it seems.

45. Ńlááhdę́ę́' inágáálígíí   t'áá éí áají' ałdo' t'áá éí   hach'i'
    From there the one that same one to also same one towards
            walks for you   there   them

kwíił'į̨. Áko t'áá áádę́ę́' kojį' awéé' bee nabizhnitin.
it   So they from to   baby by they teach.
sends.   there here   it

Héichiihígíí yá'át'ééhígíí shį̨į̨   bee nabi'di'nitin— niłch'i
The one born the good one it   by they give to   Wind
for them   seems it him instruction—

yá'át'éehii bee naho'di'nitin áají'   (C A B).
the good   by they were   over
one   it taught   there.

46. Binaadę́ę́' ałts'íísí éidíí'ígíí ńlááhdę́ę́' nihinitsékees
    From   little   that one from   our thinking
    around   there

nihii' sizínígíí díníłnahgo áko áádę́ę́' niłch'i áádę́ę́'
in us one that when it   then from Wind   from
       stands   gets tired   there   there

anéíyii'níł áko nihinitsékees bidziil, nihiyi' sizíinii
it sends   so our thinking is   in us   the one

again   strong,   standing
bidziil. Háídoodlééł jiní. Éidí kodéé' éí yaa   doo
is   It take it   t.s. That from   because not
strong out   here   of it

nihik'idagháah da. Kodóó ńlááh ha'a'aahjį' nłch'i halne'é
us it gives up.   From   there to the east   radio
                     here

nahalingo kodóó áajį' halne', díí'ígíí át'éego kodóó yáshti'ígíí
like   from   to   it   this   way   from   what I am
          here   there reports,   here   saying

át'éego k'ad áajį' diits'a'. Ákót'éego áko áadi ba náháádlá,
like   now to   it is   In that   then there it receives,
this   there heard. way   for it

áádéé' dóó k'ad, "Kót'é!" bídí'náh jiní. Kót'éego éí nitsííkees
from   next,   "This   him it t.s. In this   we think
there   way!"   tells   way

jiní (C A B).
t.s.

47. Bee hojííyá áko éí bee nitsídzíkeesgo áko há'ahwiinítįįgo
    By he gets that by when he thinks   when he is helpful
    it   wise   it

njigháago éí   ha'át'e' ádin (C L).
living   that faults he is
                lacking.

48. Díidí k'ad doo yá'át'ééhgóó yáati' da, jó kodi nii'né áko
    This now not being good   talk,   well when we   then
                                                         die

nihiiyi' sizíinii éí.... nihiiyi' hahakáh. Éí doo née da.
within   the one it... of us   walks   It not   it
us   that stands   out.   dies.

Jó éí doo yá'át'ééhgóó yáájałti'éé éí haiyi' háíyáh, éí ńláahdi
So he not being good   one who   it of him walks that over
                       spoke   out,   there

ch'įįdii nlįįgo. Áko nłch'i kodi ei ałk'idą́ą́' diné yąą kót'íi'go
Ghost   being. So Wind then it after-   per- removing it-
                                 wards   son self from

éidí kwe'é ítah   ńdii'nahgo ákogo hazaad doo yá'át'éeh da (C A B).
that then among it rises   so then one's not it is good.
           one   words

49. Jó éí díí nichǫ'ígíí éí chahałheeł yimąsii wolyé. Kojí
    This   evil one it Darkness Rolling is   This
                                          called.

nłch'i yá'át'éehii éí t'óó chahałheeł wójí. Áájí nichǫ'ógo
Wind good one it just Darkness is   There being
                             called.   evil

nitsékees jó éí bąąhágii éhooníłgo diné ádin, nidahaleehgóó
thoughts   that bad if it hap- per- dies, after that
                      pens   son

ii'háhejeehę́ę́ bił   ełteeldego át'é. Jinéł'įigo jo díí nłch'iígíí
it runs out with mixing it is. When look- this Wind
             them   ing at it

nłch'i yá'át'éehii éí shábik'ehgo náalwoł éí. Éí díí nichǫ'ígíí
Wind good one it sunwise   turns that. This evil one

ii'háhejeehę́ę́ éí shádáahjį' kót'éego náalwoł (C M).
it runs out   that sunward this way it
                                     turns.

50. Jó áko díí kwe'é binaadi naajeehii'ígíí jó díkwííshį́į́ ałą́ą
    So   these here around the ones that so many   differ-
                                   run   ent

át'éego naajeeh. Jó ła nłch'i noodǫ́ǫ́z wolyé jiní. Náánáá ła
being   run   One Wind Striped is   t.s. Again one
        around.   called

éiyá nłch'i hanoo'ts'ee' wolyé jiní. Jó áko ła' nłch'i náayis
that Wind Spiraling   is   t.s.   One Wind Revolv-
            called   ing

jó jiní. T'áá éí shį́į́ kojį' dahiilgho' yileehgo doo yá'át'éehgo
that t.s. These it to here they   if that   not good way
         seems   run   happens

njighá ho'ditnii łeh. Éí át'į́ t'áá nłch'i át'į́. Doo yá'át'ééhji
one of one it usu- It does that Wind does Not good way
walks is said ally. it   it

áí háyaat': "Kodi ní!" hałní nahalin ńlááhdę́ę́ (C A B).
it for one "This say!" to one it   from there.
  it talks   it says seems

51. Shádáahjį' náalwołgo nihik'élghod, nihii'   yilgho'go, jó áko éí
    Sunward   if it runs on us it   within if it runs, well then
                                    runs,   us

t'áá ádzaagóó nitsííkees.... Nłch'iyéę doo ákwááníł da
just any way we think....   Wind that not right it
                                    was   acts

doo akwííyoolíł da bee hinii'nánéę   nihits'ą́ą' kwííł'í (F D T).
not right it does   by we had lived ours   it does
        to it   it   to it.

52. Yá'át'éehii t'éí nihiih hilyá ndi jó ńlaahdi nikidii'nahdóó
    Good ones   only in us are but back   when we start
                              put   there crawling

áádóó nihéédayííł'in nahdinaajeehéę anájahą́ą nłch'i. Ńlááhjí
from on us they are there the ones going   Wind. Over
there   put   that ran around around   there

yá'át'éehgo nohsééłéę   ha'át'íida danchǫ́'ígíí jó yéédayííł'in jó
being good was growing some-   evil ones   are put on   so
     way   thing

kót'éego bił   jiniiyé. Áko ei t'áá doo bidéélnín da, ádin (C A B).
this way with one So then   not there is a   none.
     them grows.   cure,

53. Jó ła' t'áá édílááhgo dahdeikáh, ła' éí hazhó'ógo na'nitiin
    Some just recklessly they live, some carefully teaching

éiyá yee deíkáh. Índa ashiiké díí díkwíída asdla'dago ła' adlą́
that by they And boys these so many five being some
     it live.   drink

éí yaa nidaakai, díí ła' iiná yaa nitsidakees.... Díí
that they do,   some life about they think.... Here
                                it

nidilt'éh da doo atsohodoobéézh adlą́ yileeh....   T'áá shį́į́
one or two   very difficult   drunk become.... just it
                                                       seems

bii'   naazíinii ał'ąą ádaat'é. Éí   shį́į́ ádabił'į́ (H K).
in   they stand dif- they   They it to them
them the ones   ferent are.   seems they do.

54. Łahda nizhónígo yéiilti' łeh. Áko ńléí t'áá łahgo yáati'jí
    Some- nice way we talk gener- Then another   of
    times   ally.   way   talking

niilk'i'ígíí át'įįgo, ákogo shíí łahgo át'é saad. T'áá ṇihii'
we turn to it   so then   differ- it   the   Same within
     causing,   ent   is   words.   us.

sizínígíí t'áá éí   át'í   (C A B).
the one same one does
that stands   it.

55. Áko nahdę́ę́' nichǫ́'ígíí shį́į́ héésdah. Áko shį́į́ kodi ííyisíí
     So from   evil one   it   waits.   So   here really
        there   seems

bee jinánę́ę niilłi'   nahalingo. Áko áádę́ę́' nłch'i nchǫ́'ígíí
by   one lived stops it seems.   Then from Wind   evil one
it   there

kojí iilgho'. Kwii baahágii áda'hooníł (C M).
here runs in. This   bad   happen.
        point things

56. K'ad ła' shį́į́ nichǫ́'ǫ́gíí shį́į́ ła' hą́ą́h naazį́ éí. Jó éí ígíí
     Some   it evil one   some   on   stands. These
        seems   them

doo hats'íí ńdaohoji'áah da nahalin, áko díí ts'ídá yá'át'éehii
not well   they plan   it seems,   this very   good one
bii' sizíinii   eida t'áá ałtso   bą́ą hólǫ́ǫ ndi   (C M).
in standing it   everything on it   even.
them   it   exists

57. Jó ńlą́ą́hdę́ę́' éí há   át'į́ nłch'iígíí ńlą́ą́hdę́ę́' diné doo
     From over   it for   it   that Wind from   per- not
      there   one does   there   son

yá'át'éehgóó nitsékeesii éí t'áá diné "Ha'át'éego da ídeeshłį́ł"
good way   who thinks he that per-   "Someday   I will make"
                       son

yoo'níinii (C M).
he wishes.

58. Ńléígóó joogáałgóó yá'át'éehgo joogááł, yá'át'éehgo
     There   one is   in a good   one is   in a good
           living   way   living,   way

nitsídzíkees, nizhónígo nitsídzíkees. Áko kodę́ę́' éiyá nichǫ'ígo
one thinks,   pleasant   one   Then from   bad way
            way   thinks.   there

nitsídaakeesii,   nichǫ'ígo bee yááti'ii t'áá ałtso hwiih
those who think, bad way   by   they   everything within
                         them talk   us

néiyii'níił   áko hwiih náhályeed. Ei joogaalę́ę hats'ą́ą́'
they place so   within they   That life   from one
            us   re-run.   past

neiyiiłchǫ', nitsídzíkeesę́ę t'áá ałtso   hats'ą́ą́' neiyiiłchǫ'.
it ruins,   one's past   everything from   it ruins.
            thinking`   one

Áko t'óó bitahjigo nanináh ha'nínígí. Éí áko doo yá'áshǫǫ da (G E S).
So   just in con- you   it is said. That not is good.
         fusion   walk

59. Díí ńláahdi nłch'iígíí, díidí nahoosdzáán binłch'i nilíinii,
    These over Winds,   these Earth   its Wind the one
         there   that is,

yádiłhił binłch'i nilíinii índa jóhonaa'ái, łł'éhonaa'ái,
Sky   its Wind the one and Sun,   Moon,
                  that is

jó díí éí ts'ídá   aláahdi baa hóchi'.... Díí dį́į́'ígíí
well they real- most   about one   These four
these   ly   is stingy....

báhádzid.... Éí diné   yee hináago kodóó nichǫ'ǫgo
are dan-   This per- by   if he   from bad
gerous....   son   them lives here way

baa   nitsídzíkeesgo doo ádoníił da. Nichǫ'ǫgo nitsídzíkeesyę́ę
about thinking if not it will   In bad   that thinking
him   happen.   way

doo hak'ehgo dooleeł, t'óó hwíjíigo biyaa ezhdoołł'ish (C M).
not his way will,   mere- oneself under one will fall.
         go   ly   him

60. Díí k'ad diné ńléí yá'át'ééh nitsékeesgo, doo be'édíláahgóó,
    This here per-   it is   when he   not reckless being,
         son   good   thinks,

doo t'áá ádzaagi yááti'góó, jó éí ba'át'e' adin wolyé. Díí
not just any way he talks, well his are is called.
                                    that faults lacking this

k'ad ńléí be'édílááh da t'áá ádzaagóó yááti'go, jó éí ba'át'e'
here there reckless and just any way talking, that his
                                                              faults

hóló̧. Kodi biyi'di sizíinii shį́į́ át'éego shį́į́ ákót'é nabiłáh
exist. Here within the one it it that it leads
           him that stands being seems way him

nahalin nitsáhákees'ígíí (F D T).
it seems this thinking.

61. Nłch'i ya'at'éehii nihitah hóló̧o̧go éí shábik'ehgo nanáalwoł
    Wind the good one among existing it in sunwise turns
                             us way

ba'át'e' ádin díí nłch'i. Shádáahjį' nanáalwołii éí ba'át'e'
its is this Wind. Sunward the one it its
fault lacking that turns fault

hóló̧o̧nii át'é.
this one it
has is.

    Diné yá'át'ééh dooleełii yá'át'éehgo sizį́ dooleełii, jó éí
    Man good who will good way he one who well he
                        be stands will,

díího̧ígíí nłch'i yá'át'éehii bii' haleeh. Ba'át'e' ádinii, doo
this one Wind good one in forms. His faults he not
                        him lacks,

be'édílááhii, éí yik'ehgo bá'ahwiinít'į.... Nááná kojí
reckless one, he towards is helpful.... Again over
                        them here

diné doo bá'ahwiinít'įįgóó, doo'ídehwóláágóó yaagááł,
man not being helpful, being stubborn he walks,

niiyá'íhwodeelti', saad t'áá doo yá'ádaat'éehii jó éí yee yááti'
he criticizes, words not good ones these by he
                                            them speaks

ałdó. Éí ńláahdi nłch'i t'áá kót'éii bii' hóole'ii éí át'é (C M).
also. Back then Wind just same in formed that it is.
                        way him

62. Ńlááhdéé' nłch'i yá'át'éehii bee hadiidzihii jo áádéé'
From there Wind the good by we will   from
                   one it speak   there

nihii' hiiyiilé shį́į́, áko índa kodóó ák'ítsíhídiikees.   Áko índa
in us it puts it   so then from we think for our- And
         seems,   there   selves.

kodóó bee hahiidzih éí yiniiyé kwiih ínáágááł nłch'i áłts'íísí.
from by we speak it for that here it goes Wind the Little
then it   reason   around   One.

Índa ńlááhdéé' nchǫ'į́ nihididoot'ihii dooleełii ałdó' ńlááh
And from   bad   that affect us they will also there
    there   (ones)

nihits'ą́ąjí' kwíń'į́. T'áá   jiniił'ahági shį́į́ ákóoni' iigho'
from us   them it When it is not   it   in there it
       pushes.   watching seems   runs

jó kodóó nihąąh dadahwǫǫyii'ah. Éí kót'é   éí t'áá éí bik'ehgo
so from on us sickness is   That way that same according
   then   put.   one   to it

nitséhwiidiikees ńlááh nihilą́ąjį' ák'ítsídiilkos dóó
our thinking   there in front for ourselves and
                     of us   we think

ák'íyádiilti'. Áko kodéé' nihikéédéé' niyiileh kodéé' bee
for ourselves So from   behind us   it puts from by
we talk.   here   here   it

nihich'į́'nahwiinááshį́į́— bík'ítsíhidiilkeesgo índa adáhodiiyiit'ah.
we suffer hardship—   about it we thinking and for ourselves
                                              we plan.

Kwiih yiniiyé naagha éí   óolyé nłch'i áłts'íísí   (C A B).
Here for that it   that called Wind the Little
      reason exists   One.

63. Jó éí díí dził   bii'   dah'iike'di éí ákót'é.   Áko kwe'é nłch'i
   So these moun- in   were placed that way So here Winds
           tains them   there   it is.

nihiniiyé sinilii éí   ńlááhdéé' éí dząądi nihitah   daakai jó áko
for us   placed these from   these here among us they   you see.
                   there   walk

Doo hoł'íłįgogo diné baa   joodlohgo diné bizhi' dajile'go,
Not something per- about laugh-   per- names you call,
    you value if son   ing   son

jó áko ńláąhdę́ę́' dził   biyi' dah'iike'dę́ę́' áádę́ę́'ígíí áko áadi
then from there moun- in   placed from the ones then there
        tains   from there

hane' áadi hane' adééł'į ńláahjį'. Áko áadi índa éíga:
news there news they   to there. So over next this:
        send   there

"Kwe'é diné   kót'éego njighááhígíí kojíníílá!" Kót'éego hane'
"Here person this   he leads his this he   In this   news
        way   life   said!"   way

anáádahyii'ah éí díí nłch'i (C M).
it brings   this Wind.
    back

64. Áko yá'át'ééh joogáałgo jó áko yá'át'ééh jiní. Doo ákwii
      Good   one walks well   it is good t.s.   Not right

joogáałgóó éí jó áko éí doo bił   yá'át'ééh da jiní. Díídí k'ad
one walks that then not with it is good   t.s.   This here
                        it

nłch'i nihi dishnínígíí jó éí nitsíí'iłkees nahdę́ę́' hach'į'
Wind to you I say   that makes one from   to one
                        think   there

yáałti' nahalin, k'ad nłch'i díí. Áko nihinitsékees át'é,
it talks it   here Wind this. So our thinking   it is,
    seems,

nihinahat'a' át'é, bik'ehgo hinii'náanii át'é. Ńláąhdę́ę́' díí
our plans   it is, according we live   it is. From there this
                to it

t'áá nłch'iígíí jó t'áá éí   nihinitsékees: "T'áá ńláąh góne'
    Wind   same one our thinking: "Just there through

deesháął!" jinízǫǫ, joogáałyę́ę. Kojí da ajogháago jidiigohda,
I will   one   one walked. Over   one walks one stumbles,
walk!"   wanted,   here

jó éí doo yá'át'éeh da jiní (H B).
so that not it is good t.s.

65. Jó díí t'áá łá'ígíí nłch'i wolyéi bee dahinii'náanii
    So this that is one Wind called by the one we
                    it   live by

  ńláahdéé' doo ákót'éego joogáálgo ch'óóshdáá'dáá' t'áá haháh
  from there not right way one walks at first   saves one

  nízin nahalingo. "Hazhó'ógo joogáál, kwíínáál, kwíínáál!"   halní
  it   it seems. "Carefully walk,   walk here, walk here!" it
  wants   says

  jidigháahgo. T'áá biláahjí' nichǫ́'ígo jidigháahgo áko hanaanish
  if one starts Beyond it   bad way if one starts   it works
  this way.   for one

  biłhé, "Ńláahdéé' kót'éego dooleełyéé" ch'ééh nízingo. T'áá
  very "From back this way it should   in   thinking. In
  hard,   then   have been" vain

  ákót'éego t'óó t'áá ákót'éego náásjidigháahgo t'áá bí ńláahdéé'
  that way just in this way   again if one   it from
                             starts   then on

  jó doo áákóne' ahwiiłáah da jiní, nłch'i wolyéi (H B).
  it not through it leads   t.s., Wind the one
     here   one   called

66. Jó t'áá bíjí nłch'iígíí díí t'áá bíjí díí k'ad achiłda-
    So that its Wind this its this now each other
         way   way

  hwiilne'ígíí át'éego ahiłdahahne' jiní. Nahdéé' shíí na'ak'íí-
  we are tell- it   they tell   t.s. From   it   about him
    ing being each other   there   seems

  yááti'go. Áko "Nichǫ,t'áá doo baa nídaat'íní, bíni' yigáál,
  talking. This "No, don't   him bother, leave him
       way   alone,

  bíni' háágóó yigáál." Jó kwe'é   doo yá'áshǫǫ da (H B).
  let him do what he When this not it is
        wants."   happens   good.

67. Nłch'i nilíinii ńláahdéé' hanitsékeesgo jó ákogo
    Wind the one from there of one it   so when
        that is   thinks

honéél'įigo doo ákwii joogáálgóó kodi ha'át'íida hagáál nilíinii
at one it　　not right one walks then whatever one's the one
looks　　　　　　　　　　　　　　　　　　gait　that is

hajáád da díí hats'ááz'a'　da doo nił dzilgóó éí yił'iigo,　　kót'éego
one's and this one's ap- too not strong　　that it makes, in
legs　　　pendages　　　　　　　　　　　　　　this way

t'áá atiingóó joogáályéę doo hózhǫ́ yit'íį' da yileehgo....
on the road on was　not well it　　happens....
　　　walking　　.　　appears

Áko ńláahdi ni'kwííyił'įhgo t'áá ch'ééh nahalingo wónáásdóó
So　there　it slows it down　futile it seems　after
　　　　　　　　　　　　　　　　　　awhile

nihaa néídiidlééh jiní. T'áá kódí jiní (H B).
from　it takes it　t.s. That is all t.s.
us

68. Ts'ídá t'áá ííyiisíí adiilzihgo, jó ako doo yá'át'éehii,
　　Just　really　　if we will　some- not that is good,
　　　　　　　　　　　　err,　thing

kodi nítch'i hani' yiniiyé ndaakai. Doo yá'át'éehii bee
here Winds news for it　they　　Not good ones by
　　　　　　　　　walk.　　　　　them

haidzihgo jó ako illzih diné niidlį́į́jí.　　"Jó doo hoł　yá'át'éeh da"
if we talk well　then we err Navajo our way. "Not　with it is good"
　　　then　　　　　　　　　　　　　　him

nihi'di'niih. Ńlááhdę́ę' nihidiyin nilíinii　áko nítch'iyę́ę
about us it　From there our　　the One then Wind past
　is said.　　　　　Holy　that is

nihiyi' heilééh. Nihijéíyę́ę niłtł'i'　jiní (C A B).
in us　it takes Our heart it stops t.s.
　　　out.

69. ...Adiits'a'go át'é. Díí k'ad diné　niidlínígíí jó bee
　...listening　it is. These　Navajo we who　so by
　　　　　　　　　　　　　　are　　it

hinii'ná kodi. Áko kodóó bich'į' yéilti'. Néikąąhgo jo
we live here. So from to it　we　If we plead
　　　　here　　talk.　with it

nihidiits'a'. T'áá áko áádóó yá'át'éeh. Ha'í'da ąą dahoołaahgo
us it hears. So   then from it is good. Some- on   if it
               there   where one harms

áádóó bee yá'át'ééh yileeh. Diné náádiidá (F D T).
from by it is   comes Per- gets well.
there it good   to be. son

REFERENCES

Aberle, David F.
  1966   *The Peyote Religion Among the Navaho.* Chicago: Aldine
         Publishing Company.

Brugge, David M.
  1963   *Navajo Pottery and Ethnohistory.* Window Rock, Arizona:
         Navajoland Publications, Navajo Tribal Museum.

Curtis, Edward S.
  1907   *The North American Indian.* Cambridge, U.S.A.: The
         University Press.

Fishler, Stanley A.
  1953   *In the Beginning: A Navaho Creation Myth. University of Utah
         Anthropological Papers,* No. 13, Salt Lake City.

Franciscan Fathers
  1910   *An Ethnologic Dictionary of the Navaho Language.*
         St. Michaels, Arizona: St. Michaels Press.

Goddard, Pliny E.
  1933   *Navajo Texts. Anthropological Papers of the American Museum of Natural History* 34:127–179.

Haile, Berard
  1939   *Blessingway, Version II, Told by Frank Mitchell, Chinle, Arizona.* Manuscript 112–5, Museum of Northern Arizona, Flagstaff.

  1932a   *Blessingway, Version I, Told by Slim Curly, Crystal, New Mexico.* Manuscript 112–4, Museum of Northern Arizona, Flagstaff.

  1932b   *Chiricahua Windway of the Navaho. Chíshí (Biṅłch'iji), Told by Tódók'óji, Salt Water Man of Lukachukai, Arizona.* Manuscripts 63–19 (English Translation) and 63–20 (Navajo Text), Museum of Northern Arizona, Flagstaff.

  1932c   *Navaho Windway Ceremony, Told by Dagha Náshjin (Black Mustache) of Chinlee, Arizona.* Manuscripts 63–21 (English Translation) and 63–22 (Navajo Text), Museum of Northern Arizona, Flagstaff.

  1933a   *Chiricahua Windway, Told by Slim Curly.* Manuscripts 63–17 (English Translation) and 63–18 (Navajo Text), Museum of Northern Arizona, Flagstaff.

  1933b   *The Holy Way of the Red Ant Chant, Told by Hastiin Dijoolí (White Cone).* Manuscript 63–15, Museum of Northern Arizona, Flagstaff.

  1938   *Navaho Chantways and Ceremonials. American Anthropologist* 40:639–652.

  1943   *Soul Concepts of the Navaho. Annali Lateranensi,* Vol. VII. Città del Vaticano.

  1951   *A Stem Vocabulary of the Navajo Language. English-Navaho,* Vol. II. St. Michaels, Arizona: St. Michaels Press.

  n.d.a   *Blessingway, Version III, Told by River Junction Curly.* Manuscript 112–6, Museum of Northern Arizona, Flagstaff.

  n.d.b   *Where People Moved Opposite (Text Dictated by Curly Tó aheedlíinii of Chinle, Arizona).* Manuscript 63–5 (English Translation) and 63–6 (Navajo Text), Museum of Northern Arizona, Flagstaff.

Horton, Robin
 1967   African Traditional Thought and Western Science. Part I.
        From Tradition to Science. *Africa* 37:50–71.

Kay, Paul
 1966   Ethnography and the Theory of Culture. *Buckness Review*
        14: 106–113.

Klah, Hasteen
 1942   *Navajo Creation Myth, The Story of the Emergence.* Recorded
        by Mary C. Wheelwright. *Navajo Religion Series*, Vol. I.
        Museum of Navajo Ceremonial Art, Santa Fe.

Kluckhohn, Clyde
 1949   The Philosophy of the Navaho Indians. In *Ideological
        Differences and World Order.* F.S.C. Northup, Ed. New
        Haven: Yale University Press.

Ladd, John
 1957   *The Structure of a Moral Code.* Cambridge: Harvard Univer-
        sity Press.

Lévi-Strauss, Claude
 1966   *The Savage Mind.* Chicago: University of Chicago Press.

Lévy-Bruhl, Lucien
 1971   *The "Soul" of the Primitive.* Chicago: Henry Regnery.

Luckert, Karl W.
 1975   *The Navajo Hunter Tradition.* Tucson: The University of
        Arizona Press.

Lyons, John
 1968   *Introduction to Theoretical Linguistics.* Cambridge, England:
        Cambridge University Press.

Matthews, Washington
 1897   *Navajo Legends.* Boston: Houghton, Mifflin and Company.

Mischel, Walter
 1968   *Personality and Assessment.* New York: Wiley.

O'Bryan, Aileen
 1956   The Diné: Origin Myth of the Navaho Indians. *Bureau of
        American Ethnology Bulletin* No. 163. Washington, DC.:
        Smithsonian Institution.

Radin, Paul
   1957   *Primitive Man as Philosopher.* (2nd Revised Ed.) New York:
           Dover.

Reichard, Gladys A.
   1943   Human Nature as Conceived by the Navajo Indians.
           Review of Religion 7:353–360.

   1970   *Navaho Religion. A Study of Symbolism.* (2nd Ed.) New York:
           Pantheon.

Spencer, Katherine
   1947   Reflection of Social Life in the Navaho Origin Myth.
           University of New Mexico Publications in Anthropology.
           Albuquerque: New Mexico Press.

Stephen, A. M.
   1930   Navajo Origin Legend. *Journal of American Folklore* 43:88–
           104.

Walker, J. R.
   1917   The Sun Dance and Other Ceremonies of the Oglala Divi-
           sion of the Teton Dakota. *Anthropological Papers of the
           American Museum of Natural History,* Vol. 16, Part II:51–221.

Werner, Oswald
   1967   Systematized Lexicography or "Ethnoscience." The Use of
           Computer Made Concordances. *The American Behavioral
           Scientist* 10(5):5–8.

Werner, Oswald, with Hagedorn W., Roth, G., Scheppers, E., and
Uriate, L.
   1969   *Some New Developments in Ethnosemantics* (Note I). Manu-
           script, Northwestern University.

Wheelwright, Mary C.
   1949   Emergence Myth According to the Hanelthnayhe or
           Upward-Reaching Rite. Museum of Navajo Ceremonial
           Art, Santa Fe.

Witherspoon, Gary
   1974   The Central Concepts of Navajo World View. Part I.
           Linguistics 119:41–59.

   1977   *Language and Art in the Navajo Universe.* Ann Arbor: The
           University of Michigan Press.

Wyman, Leland C.
    1962   *The Windways of the Navaho.* The Taylor Museum of the
            Colorado Fine Arts Center, Colorado Springs.

    1970   *Blessingway. With Three Versions of the Myth Recorded and
            Translated from the Navajo by Father Berard Haile, O.F M.*
            Tucson: The University of Arizona Press.

Wyman, Leland C., Hill, W. W., and Ósanai, Iva
    1942   Navajo Eschatology. *The University of New Mexico Bulletin,*
            No. 377. Albuquerque: University of New Mexico Press.

Wyman, Leland C., and Kluckhohn, Clyde
    1938   Navaho Classification of Their Song Ceremonials. *Memoirs,*
            American Anthropological Association, No. 50.

INDEX